If Protestantism is True

Devin Rose

If Protestantism is True

The Reformation Meets Rome

Unitatis Books

Dedication

To my wife, Catherine, for her tireless support and encouragement with this book and with all my projects.

Contents

Acknowledgments

I owe many people thanks for directly or indirectly helping me in bringing this book to fruition. To Catherine, my loving wife, who juggled our four young children for hours on end while I worked on the manuscript. To Betsy Stokes, for her thoughtful editing. To Tekeme Studios, for designing the book's cover and website. To all my Protestant brothers and sisters in Christ, through whom I came to know Jesus and who have patiently engaged with me in dialogue about these important issues. To all my Catholic friends and family, for encouraging me in my faith. To blog readers, facebook friends, podcast subscribers, for your years of faithful reading, listening, and support. For their wit and wisdom, as well as the inspiration for the book's subtitle, I want to thank the contributors of Called to Communion (www.calledtocommunion.com). Finally, none of this would matter were it not for Jesus Christ, our Lord and King.

Chapter One
A Search for Truth

I believe and profess all that the Holy Catholic Church teaches and proclaims to be revealed by God.

But it was not always so. I grew up secularly. My mother was brought up in a particularly legalistic branch of the churches of Christ denomination, and my father, in the Episcopal Church. But the only church I remember going to as a child was a Unitarian Universalist one, and we went there for just a short time. The sole Unitarian sermon I recall having to sit through included a joke about (then Vice President) Dan Quayle that got big laughs from the congregation. I was taught at home and at school that humans evolved without purpose from primordial ooze, so unsurprisingly, when I became old enough to reason about such things, I proudly declared that I did not believe in God.

In high school, I came to base the perception of my own worth as a person on what others thought of me. It was an unstable foundation to be sure, but so long as everyone thought well of me and I had nothing to be humiliated about, all was well. Eventually however, this way of thinking caught up with me, and I reached a point where I could not hide any longer from it. That point came during my sophomore year in college. On the outside, my life was really great: I made good grades in school and had a nice girlfriend, a family who loved me, and lots of friends. But on the inside, I was beginning to be eaten alive by anxiety. It started out small and slowly got worse. I began getting nervous in social situations like going to restaurants, to the movies, and eventually, just being in class for school. My stomach would churn, and I would fear having to run out of the classroom, embarrassing myself in front of everyone.

Other humiliating aspects from these disordered anxieties began to surface: when I felt really anxious, I would begin noticeably sweating, for no apparent reason. And when the anxieties became really bad, I would have panic attacks, where my heart would start beating frantically, and my fears would feed into one another in a spiraling cycle that I could not control. I did a good job of hiding my anxieties from others, bottling all of it inside and trying to "think" my way out of the fears.

During my junior year, I was interning for a semester and living with my mother, and I began having headaches every day. This persisted for five months solid. They wore down what little physical and emotional strength I had left within me, and near the end of my internship, I was driving home each day hoping that a car would swerve into my lane and kill me. Here I was, an honor student, full-scholarship holder, and a talented athlete surrounded by good friends and family, and I had reached a point where I wanted to die rather than suffer through another day of hiding my problems. It was at that point that I faced for the first time what my atheistic beliefs really meant: despair. Always before in my life, the thin veneer of comfort, prosperity, and general well-being had protected me from facing the terrifying existential conclusions of my worldview. One day, in a disturbing waking dream, I saw before me total, empty blackness—a vivid manifestation of my utter hopelessness.

Finally I told my mother about my anxieties. (I thank God now that even in despair, He gave me a loving mother to whom I could turn when I thought that I had nowhere else to go.) She suggested that I see a psychologist, which humiliated me further, because I had always looked with disdain upon people who went to psychologists. To my great relief, however, the psychologist helped me realize that my condition was not unique. She taught me some cognitive behavioral therapy techniques, including breathing exercises and positive thinking. These helped, but only in a limited way. My anxieties persisted almost as strongly as ever, and I realized then that I was in trouble: I was clinically depressed, suffering from frequent panic attacks, and fighting a titanic struggle with never-ending anxieties. I believed that my problems were just chemicals in my brain, but I had tried every tactic that I could think of to beat the anxiety, and none had worked. My once-reliable intelligence now failed me utterly, so I faced a choice: either commit suicide or try to believe in God. For some reason, that was the dichotomy in my heart, even after years as an ardent atheist.

I decided to try belief first, with suicide as the backup plan. I knew that if God did not exist, then "trying" to believe in him would not work, because it would just be me trying one more mental tactic among the multitude that I had already tried without any success. But if God *did* exist, then I shouldn't kill myself without giving Him a fair shake. Still, the stupidity of asking God for help revolted me. But with nothing to lose, I gave it a try. I began praying for the first time ever by saying, "God, you know I do not believe in you, but I am in trouble and need help. If you are real, help me." I also started reading the Bible to learn about Christianity, starting with Genesis, for I was determined to begin at the beginning.

The initial result of my prayers was, well, *nothing.* I didn't see God or Jesus or anything supernatural. No one whispered anything in my ear. If I had an angel, he didn't come to visibly embrace me and kick my demons out. My problems didn't go away, nor did they seem to lessen noticeably. This disappointing result did not surprise me but instead wryly confirmed what I had always believed: "God doesn't exist, so thinking He'll help you is foolish." But when you are in the ocean and all you have is a life preserver, however small it may be, it's the only hope that you've got. So I kept asking God for help every day and kept reading the Bible, though the King James Version with its "thees" and "thous" and "begats" made for near-inscrutable study. Slowly, however, under this simple regimen of prayer and reading, things began improving slightly, enough for me to notice a difference. Once, a picture formed in my mind of a little sapling in the woods, overshadowed by huge trees. I knew that this sapling represented my faith in God: tiny, vulnerable, frail. All my beliefs sought to destroy the sapling: atheism, atheistic evolution, the absurdity of believing in God, and the doubts that some invisible being could help me. So I protected the sapling in my mind, knowing that I had to give it a chance to grow, that it was the only possible lifeline I had. When my thoughts rebelled against belief in God or assaulted me with a myriad of doubts while reading the Bible, I pushed those thoughts aside, suspending the disbelief and exerting myself to believe, all the while telling God that He had better help me if He valued my life at all.

When I returned to college after my internship, I lived with a friend of mine who was a faithful Baptist, and he took me to church with him each Sunday. It was a strange experience, being around people who were singing songs to God and praying together. My social anxiety disorder made it tough for me to sit anywhere in the church without feeling very anxious. I didn't know the songs or the prayers, and so I felt even more like an outsider. Still, I persevered. I continued reading the Bible, asking my roommate questions about what I was reading, and praying. Slowly (and amazingly) over the course of several months, my faith grew appreciably, and it eventually threatened to whelm my doubts and unbelief. It was incredible and something that I knew I could not have manufactured. As the months went by in my senior year of college, I deepened my friendships with the Christians I knew, attended church and Sunday school regularly, and started calling myself a Christian.

At some point that year, the scales tipped, and God came rushing in. It was like nothing I had ever experienced. I was given the courage and strength to face my crippling anxieties and to begin to overcome them. I read the entire Bible from cover to cover and then began reading it again, along with other spiritual books. God had given me hope to counter my despair, and faith and love began to heal my deep wounds. I encountered Jesus Christ for the first time and was finally able to receive the love that He had longed to give me for so many years. Jesus Christ, the Lord of the universe—who created the laws of physics in His brilliance and yet became a human being to rescue me from my sinful, selfish, meaningless way of living—loved me and had created me to love Him forever.

I didn't see a flash of light; I never heard Christ's voice, and I never saw Jesus or the Holy Spirit. But I believed in Him and believed that all He said in the Bible was true. As I grew to learn His teachings and commands, I realized that He desires only what is good for us and that He alone knows what will fulfill us. I felt God taking a hold of me and my life changing dramatically. Finally, near the end of my senior year, I was baptized in the Baptist church and became a member of it. I believed in Jesus Christ. I believed that the Bible was the inerrant word of God. I had become, though I would not have called myself this, an Evangelical Protestant, and my spiritual life had begun.

Anywhere but the Catholic Church

So how then did I come to be Catholic? I had just been baptized in the spring of my senior year in college and was growing tremendously in my faith. I was involved in Bible studies, went to a young men's fellowship group, and volunteered with disadvantaged elementary-school children. I also began memorizing Scripture verses.

I had one summer and one fall semester left before graduating from college. Most of my friends left town for the summer and went back home to work, often in youth ministry at Evangelical churches. But one of my friends, Matt, was staying in town to take classes, so he and I roomed together for the summer. We went to church together regularly and frequently talked about our Christian faith. He was a logical thinker and a good debater, so we could delve into matters deeply and have lively discussions without taking things personally if we disagreed.

I had begun to grow uneasy about why we as Christians were so divided from each other in our teachings and in our worship. Our Southern Baptist beliefs differed, on big and small matters, from those of other denominations, and we certainly didn't worship with them. They had their church, and we had ours. Our (very large) Baptist church was only a short distance away from an equally large Presbyterian one, a troubling example of our intra-Christian divisions. "What do they believe at that Presbyterian church?" I asked Matt. But he didn't know either.

That first question began a long series of discussions that we had together about the lack of Christian unity and whether it was a problem. It got me thinking about what I believed about God and more importantly, why I believed it. I had only been a Christian for one short year (and had only been baptized for a few months), but already I more or less subscribed to the Southern Baptist teachings and had rejected conflicting beliefs held by other denominations. How had I, a newly minted Christian, come so quickly to a conclusion about which denomination taught the most accurate truth?

I realized then that all I had learned about Christianity came from an Evangelical Protestant perspective. My friends had promptly bought me a large, well-annotated, New International Version of the Bible to replace my King James Version. I read this Bible from cover to cover and read it again. When I didn't understand something, which was often, I would look down and see if there was an explanatory note about it, and I usually found one. This feature is very helpful, but I realize now that the answers were all interpretations through an Evangelical Protestant lens. When I had questions about the Faith, I would ask my Evangelical friends, and they would answer me according to what they believed was true.

These are not bad things. They are the ordinary way that God made us and account for why children of Muslims usually become Muslim, children of Christians become Christian, and so on. However, I needed to survey other Christian denominations' beliefs and decide for myself what was true. So I returned to the discussions with my friend Matt about which denomination's teachings were "closest" to the truth that God has revealed, praying that Jesus would guide me. Because having now discovered Him, I wanted to be as close to Him as possible.

I assumed that the Bible was the sure basis for truth, because we believed it was the inerrant word of God. That sounded good, but there were two problems: firstly, other Protestant denominations claimed the same thing, and yet we were divided from them in our beliefs, and secondly, the Catholic Church claimed there were seven more books, not included in our Bibles, which were inspired by God.

The first problem led to the inevitable conclusion that it was possible for different Christians—all claiming to be "led by the Holy Spirit" and all basing their beliefs on "the Bible alone"—to veer off in different, mutually exclusive directions. Throughout history, I discovered, some person or group within a Protestant church came to believe differently than the others and broke off to form their own, new denomination. This seemed to me to violate Christ's prayer and command for us Christians to be in unity (see John 17). The Holy Spirit is the Spirit of Truth and would never lead people to believe something untrue, so that meant that at least some of the Christians who thought they were listening accurately to the Spirit's promptings were in reality, not.

The second problem was of a different sort, because it struck at the root of the tree of my faith: we believed in the "Bible alone," yet that meant we had to know with confidence which books made up the Bible! Here we had the Catholic Church claiming that my Bible was missing seven books that God had inspired and therefore desired to be included. How did I know who was right? More broadly, who had determined which books should be in the Bible, when did they do so, and why should I believe them?

I finally concluded at that point that one of two things must be true: either the Holy Spirit had *tried* to guide Christians to know which books belonged in the Bible, but we may still have gotten some of the books wrong, *or* the Holy Spirit by God's grace succeeded, miraculously overcoming our myriad faults, such that the Bible was made up of the exact books that God himself inspired.

In other words, God either preserved His Church throughout history from errors which would corrupt her teachings, or He did not, leaving us in a state where we could only be *somewhat* confident that *most* of our beliefs were *hopefully* true.

I was hoping that God *had* preserved His Church from errors in her teachings, so I wondered: which denominations had the boldness to claim that they were that Church who held the fullness of the truth? (My Baptist church certainly didn't claim that.) It turned out that Catholics, Orthodox, and Mormons claimed that. The two of these that had credible claims historically and theologically were the Catholic Church and the Orthodox Churches—both were a long way from my Evangelical Protestantism.

I was dumbfounded and unsettled. The Catholic Church taught things about Mary, purgatory, the saints, the sacraments, and priests that I thought were completely bogus. But I tried to set this bias aside and be objective. With a sense of dread, I began investigating the Catholic Church in earnest, looking and hoping for something that would let me off the hook to return to Protestantism in peace.

Alas, I failed to find it. I challenged my Evangelical friends to prove my arguments wrong and explain where I was going off course. They tried to do so but could not explain, for example, why I should accept the Protestant canon of Scripture (or any canon for that matter). For months, we debated many matters of our Faith, but I returned again and again to the canon of Scripture and the authority by which it was formed. For many of my friends who had been raised in the Faith, my stubborn questioning was hard to fathom. But the freshness of my conversion, perhaps, kept my curiosity ignited.

I studied books, took part in internet discussions, and read stories of faithful and intelligent Protestants converting to the Catholic Faith. I joined RCIA (the Rite of Christian Initiation for Adults—an odd-sounding name for the classes you take if you are thinking of becoming Catholic) in the last semester of my senior year and was received into the Catholic Church at Easter of 2001. Two of my Evangelical friends, including Matt, came to the four-hour-long vigil Mass. I greatly respect and love my Protestant friends; I would not be the new man that I am today without them.

My anxieties didn't disappear in the blink of an eye. Instead, they slowly diminished as God replaced my atheistic, selfish worldview with the truth. I learned that I was a child of God and that my worth as a person stemmed from that and not from what others thought of me. I learned to respect myself and others more deeply than I ever could have as an atheist. I now lean on Christ daily for strength to face my fears, and though they still surface at times, they no longer rule my life—God does.

My "road to Rome," then, began with taking the risk that God might be real. It continued with the discovery that He loved me and was worth trusting. And as I trusted Him, I felt confident enough to question myself—including my Protestant perspective. This book is a discussion of that time of questioning and the answers that I have found after ten years of reflection.

A Note About Terminology

The Catholic Church considers the Orthodox Churches to rightfully be called *Churches*—since they have preserved Apostolic Succession and the sacraments—and considers Protestant churches or particular denominations to be *ecclesial communities* as they do not (and do not claim) to do so. So I will use that nomenclature and avoid using "denomination" to describe any Christian Church or community. Sometimes I will use the phrase "Christian tradition" to refer generically to one's particular Church or community. The capitalized "Tradition" refers to the sacred or apostolic Tradition of the Catholic Church, which both preserves the full deposit of faith that Christ gave to the Apostles and through the liturgy connects us to the sacramental life of the Church. From the perspective of the Catholic Church, Protestants are Christians by virtue of their valid Trinitarian baptisms; therefore, they are rightly called brothers in Christ, though separated because of the sad divisions between us.

Protestantism Then and Now

Protestantism refers to all communities descended from the diverse set of movements that arose in Europe in the 1500s as a reaction against problems and abuses in the Catholic Church. The hallmarks of Protestantism are the doctrines of *sola Scriptura* (the Bible alone), *sola fide* (that man is made righteous before God through faith alone), and the priesthood of all believers (understood to mean that ordained clergy have no status which marks them as different from all other Christians).

Martin Luther, who unintentionally launched the Protestant Reformation in the early sixteenth century, was a German priest in a Catholic religious order. The rigor of his religious life and an unbalanced focus on doing works of penance, coupled with his tendency to be overly scrupulous, led to his rebellion and ultimate rejection of the Catholic Church's authority. Instead, his interpretation of the Bible led him to believe that we are justified by grace alone through faith alone. Interestingly, these theological ideas are not far off from the Catholic Church's teachings, which also recognize that Christians are justified by grace through faith, but the spiritual climate in Germany during Luther's day obscured these teachings. It should be noted that modern Protestant beliefs, while influenced largely by Luther's biblical interpretations, often diverge from those of Luther. But the arguments in this book will focus on Luther's ideas which most Protestants *have* accepted and incorporated into their own set of beliefs.

Protestantism started as the well-intentioned effort to correct errors and abuses in the Catholic Church, at a time when the Church was sorely in need of reform. The Catholic Church today has recognized that several Protestant beliefs contain much truth in them, and in the late twentieth-century even signed a joint declaration with large Lutheran communities on the issue of justification.

About Indulgences

Indulgences were a sticking point for Luther, and they remain so today for most Protestants. Although the concept of punishment for forgiven sins might seem foreign and scandalous to a modern-day Protestant, it isn't as graceless as it might sound at first. It is quite equivalent to the (modern) Protestant idea of being purified of the wayward desires that originally led to the sin. It is the third step in holiness, following confession of sin and forgiveness of it. See 1 John 1:9: "confess . . . forgive . . . and cleanse. . . ." The Catechism of the Catholic Church emphasizes clearly that "these two punishments [eternal in hell or temporal in purgatory] must not be conceived as a kind of vengeance inflicted by God from without, but as following from the very nature of sin. A conversion [confession and receiving forgiveness] which proceeds from a fervent charity [love for God and others] can attain the complete purification of the sinner in such a way that no punishment would remain."[1] Luther's attack on the *sale of* indulgences, then, was well warranted. Although it can be argued that someone willing to pay money in restitution for her harm to others by her sin might be showing evidence of "fervent charity," she might also simply be rich and scared of purgatory. Catholics today, then, are encouraged to use their money for God's glory however the Holy Spirit leads them and to seek their own purification through God's many means of grace. Indulgences are no longer sold—that was an abuse that was corrected—but the theology of restitution behind them has never changed.

The Purpose of This Book

The era of deep distrust and misunderstanding between Protestants and Catholics is coming to an end, fueled by the advent of the internet and the globe-shrinking power of electronic communications and media. More than ever before, it is now possible to discover what a particular Church or community teaches, how those beliefs originated, and even interact with adherents to those beliefs.

Protestants and Catholics now live and work together side-by-side, and the mutual respect that this engenders cannot but help to build the trust needed to be truly open to one another.

This book is written to help overcome, by God's grace, the sad divisions within Christianity. We know that Christ wants us unified in the truth and desires that no one believe something false about our Faith, so we can ask questions with the utmost confidence that God will supply us the necessary grace to become unified. However, He also asks us to make every effort, even to a heroic degree, to study, pray, and dialogue with one another in order to achieve this unity.

Jesus prayed to our Father for our oneness:

> And now I am no more in the world, but they are in the world, and I am coming to thee. Holy Father, keep them in thy name, which thou hast given me, that they may be one, even as we are one....I do not pray for these only, but also for those who believe in me through their word, that they may all be one; even as thou, Father, art in me, and I in thee, that they also may be in us, so that the world may believe that thou hast sent me. The glory which thou hast given me I have given to them, that they may be one even as we are one, I in them and thou in me, that they may become perfectly one, so that the world may know that thou hast sent me and hast loved them even as thou has loved me. [John 17:11,20–23, RSV].

Paul similarly exhorted Christians: "I appeal to you, brethren, by the name of our Lord Jesus Christ, that all of you agree and that there be no dissensions among you, but that you be united in the same mind and the same judgment" (1 Cor. 1:10, RSV).

What will it take for us to answer Paul's appeal and be reunited? Firstly, it will take humility on the part of every Christian. Secondly, it will require mutual respect for one another. Finally, it will take an honest examination of our beliefs, their origins, and the reasons behind them, and a willingness to be shown something more fully true than what we currently believe. I know first-hand how hard this is. I never dreamed I would become a theist. Much less a Christian.

Much less a Catholic. But then I never dreamed how satisfying it could be.

Chapter Two
A Call to Honest Self-Examination

"Faced with the choice between changing one's mind and proving that there is no need to do so, almost everyone gets busy on the proof." —John Kenneth Galbraith

The Difficulty of Conversion

Once we as human beings accept something as true, our first inclination when it is challenged is to defend that belief. This normal response is necessary for surviving in the world. If we were ready at the drop of a hat to up and discard our beliefs on everything we have accepted as true, we would live in a constant state of instability. Instead, it often takes a crisis in our life to cause us to reexamine our beliefs and whether they "work" or not. Even without a crisis, however, God has placed in us a desire to know Him who is the Truth. And so in humility, we seek the truth, trusting Christ to help us (see Matt. 7:7). This search can either show us that our current beliefs are the most truthful ones or possibly expose us to something greater.

Inertia is the thing from Newtonian physics that makes it a good idea to wear your seat belt in a moving car (because a body in motion tends to stay in motion, even when the car abruptly stops moving). There is an inertia associated with a person's principles and beliefs, too. He resists changing direction when he is considering conversion, say, to Christianity, or more specifically, to the Catholic Church. When I became convinced that the Catholic Church's claims to God-given authority were true, I literally wept when I contemplated the betrayal that my Evangelical friends would feel when I told them, and I had been an Evangelical Protestant for only one year. How much more difficult is it, then, for a person who has spent *her entire life* in a particular Protestant community to convert to Catholicism? When you combine this obstacle with the fact that our family members, friends, and associates are often strongly tied to our faith communities, you can begin to understand how difficult it can be to even consider converting. Some converts even face being ostracized by family and friends. This anticonversion inertia is impossible to overcome, but by God's grace.

The Subtlety of Bias

In order to honestly examine arguments challenging the veracity of our particular beliefs, we must first recognize the bias from our own Christian tradition (often also the one of our upbringing). For example, there are some beliefs common to the Protestant tradition (such as *sola Scriptura*, the Bible alone). But we can also speak more specifically of an *Evangelical* Protestant tradition which holds, for instance, that infant baptism is invalid. This Evangelical Protestant tradition differs from the Lutheran or Anglican Protestant traditions. There are also particular beliefs within even the Evangelical Protestant tradition: some Baptists believe that women can and should be pastors of churches; other Baptists believe that only men should be pastors.

Picture this image of a common scenario: Southern Baptist Rachel is invited to her friend's American Baptist church, but she realizes after the music portion of the service that *a woman* is getting up to give the sermon because she is the pastor of the church. Rachel's mind and heart rebel at this notion, because she has been taught and believes that it is wrong for a woman to be a pastor; it is against God's will. Afterwards, she goes home and finds the Bible verses that (by her interpretation) definitively prove that women should not be pastors, including "I do not permit a woman to teach or to have authority over a man; she must be silent" (1 Tim. 2:12, NIV). In Rachel's mind, the American Baptists are clearly going against what the Bible teaches, and she believes that her discomfort during the service was a movement of the Holy Spirit confirming that women should not be pastors.

Consider another scenario: Roman Catholic Joseph goes for the first time to his friend's Evangelical Bible church, but when he enters the sanctuary he thinks he has come to the wrong place. It looks like a theater, with a stage, a modern sound system, and auditorium seating. There are no Christian symbols to be found anywhere: no cross, no baptismal font, certainly no statues, stained glass windows, or candles. "What is going on here?" he wonders. "Is this even a church?" His mind rebels at the starkness and the lack of anything visibly Christian in the church, as well as at what he perceives to be a song-and-dance show as the service starts, with a polished singer leading the worship from the stage while the (talented) band rocks away on the drums and guitars. Joseph may not know specific passages in the Bible that would say this type of worship is wrong, but it doesn't sit right with him, because it is quite different from the meditative Catholic liturgy he is accustomed to. He feels uncomfortable and takes that to indicate that this style of worship is not what God desires.

Finally, imagine a Pentecostal Protestant attending a Catholic friend's confirmation Mass. The priest, deacons, lectors, acolytes, and altar servers process in with incense filling the air, while Gregorian music is played. Then the parishioners are standing, sitting, kneeling, then standing again. The priest says something, and everyone in the congregation responds in unison. An elderly lady across the pew is silently praying with a string of beads. It is all so foreign that the Pentecostal Christian cannot help but feel confused and displaced.

The knee-jerk reaction of a Christian attending a service of a different tradition than his own cannot, then, be immediately trusted as coming from the Holy Spirit. It likely stems from beliefs *implicitly* accepted long ago. He also likely accepted the entire tradition from which these beliefs came. He might not realize the origins of a particular belief, who decided it, and if the current belief is even still reflective of original intentions.

How, then, can we make an honest, unbiased assessment of our own Christian tradition? It begins with a Christian praying for God's help to recognize her own tradition by asking herself how she came to believe as incontrovertibly true those tenets of her faith. She then needs to ask the next question: "When and from whom did this belief first originate within Christianity?" It is naïve to assume that it was always believed just as she believes it or that "it is obviously clear" from some passage of the Bible. Rather, through prayer and study, the Christian comes to understand why she believes what she does as well as what other Christians believe and why.

The honest response is to make a concerted effort to prayerfully study these subjects while taking into account our bias toward our own tradition.

Is Truth Accessible to All?

Here is a common occurrence: we listen to one person's arguments against a belief system, and they seem quite compelling. Good-sounding reasons are given and enough challenges are fired off that even a committed follower can seriously begin to doubt whether his church is what it claims to be. Then, we listen to an apologist's arguments *for* the beliefs, and they are so convincing that we wonder how we ever could have believed the other person's case. In short, we can be swayed by a decent-sounding argument when proposed by an articulate proponent.

So what are we to do? We could throw our hands up in the air in hopelessness, for if C.S. Lewis and Martin Luther and Mother Teresa all came to different conclusions on what to believe, what hope do we have of finding the truth? I would answer that, if we had no divine help, we *would* be up a creek without a paddle, left to use what meager intelligence we could muster to figure it out for ourselves. But fortunately, we do have divine help. The God of truth wants us to know the truth!

As a Catholic, I do believe that there is a visible Church that Christ established and that God does want us to be in full communion with her. If that claim is true, then God can lead even someone who is not that gifted in intelligence or understanding to her. He has always preferred the lowly to show forth His power and love, and He has always chosen the weak to shame the strong. And so, each person has his own particular challenges and gifts when seeking the fullness of the truth. Tom Brown, a Reformed Protestant who became Catholic after years of discernment, made an insightful observation on this subject:

> I've wondered about this: what would I think of a truth
> that was only available to really smart people; or a truth
> that was not open to really smart people but only to the
> "humble of mind?" But I think I've had things mixed up

in my mind. Sure Calvin and Aquinas and Therese of Lisieux were all capable of intelligent arguments, and all smarter than I am. But does that mean that I am incapable of reaching a conclusion on truth? Is this like standing in the floodwaters of truth, and only if one is tall enough will one be able to endure the truth? I don't think so. I've come to the conclusion that even the "simple minded" can listen to opposing arguments, break them down to their fundamentals, and see which side has a challenge on the table which the other side is unable to address. I think intelligence really implicates how *long* it takes someone to process complexities, but it does not implicate an on/off ability to digest something complex.

I say all this because I used to be discouraged: people smarter than me had devoted their lives to the pursuit of truth, so what hope did I have of getting it right? But through prayer and (slow) reflection, I was able to see a consistent pattern of one side making points the other side could not rebut, but would dart away from. So I hope your friends could be encouraged, trusting in God and seeking patience in their intellectual pursuit.[1]

It would be a cruel God indeed who required some high level of intelligence in order to come to know him in the fullness of the truth. All Christians believe in a God who is kind, merciful, and loving. We know that He would neither exclude from the kingdom nor from His Church those of us who are less than geniuses. Rather, He guides each of us along the path in which we can enter through the narrow gate to Heaven (see Matt. 7:13–14).

Chapter Three
The Catholic Church in History

Let us now consider the evidence for the claim that the Catholic Church is the same Church that Christ founded and upon which His promises still rest. These first arguments will examine several aspects of the Church throughout history and consider whether they make sense if Protestantism is true.

Ecumenical Councils

Ecumenical (or general) councils have been held in Christ's Church since the Apostolic Age (first century). We see the precedent and pattern for these councils in Acts 15, the Council of Jerusalem. The Church was posed with the question of whether Gentile converts to the Christian faith needed to be circumcised in order to be saved. In preparation for the council, Paul and Barnabas "had no small dissension and debate with them [Judaizers]," and so they were "appointed to go up to Jerusalem to the Apostles and the elders about this question [of circumcision]" (Acts 15:2). After much debate among the Apostles and elders, Peter stood and explained how God gave the Holy Spirit to the Gentiles and that salvation comes by grace through faith, and not by following the Mosaic law. The Apostles then drafted a letter to be sent out to the churches in which the men making these challenges were rebuked as having gone out *without the authority of the Apostles*. The decisions made by the council were then decreed, beginning with the authoritative formula, "It has seemed good to the Holy Spirit and to us." Note that the Church primarily settled this matter by reference to the Apostles' God-given authority within the Church and not by reliance on the Old Testament—which was at best unclear on this matter, both requiring circumcision and foreshadowing Gentile salvation—or the New Testament, since only a few of the letters which would become part of the canon had even been written by this time.[1]

The next ecumenical council to be convened was at Nicaea in the year 325. It was attended by over three hundred bishops, including Hosius, bishop of Cordova and Pope Sylvester's representative (or "legate"). The primary purpose of the council was to determine whether the teachings of Arius, a deacon from Alexandria who denied the divinity of Christ and His consubstantial relationship with God the Father, were truth or heresy. Arius was an intelligent and charismatic man, and he had attracted a large following. Many bishops at the Council of Nicaea were initially supportive of him and his ideas; however, once Arius's teachings were read aloud before the bishops, they were declared heretical. The truths of Christ's divinity and of Jesus being consubstantial ("same substance" or "one in being") with the Father were consequently confirmed as dogmas.

These truths of the Faith were not invented in 325 by the bishops of Christ's Church. Rather they were always known in the deposit of faith, which consisted of the unwritten Tradition as well as the written sacred Scriptures. The Council of Nicaea only reaffirmed the truth and elevated it to the level of dogma, which meant that this teaching was an essential and unchangeable doctrine of the Christian Faith, to be believed and assented to as truth by all the faithful. Just like at the Council of Jerusalem, the bishops at Nicaea—as successors to the Apostles—made a binding decision based on the full deposit of faith, which included the unwritten Tradition. It was necessary to do so, because Arius and his followers had developed their own interpretations of Scripture passages that they were using to support their position. Who had the authority to interpret Scripture truthfully? The Council of Nicaea, following the example of the Council of Jerusalem, showed that the leaders of Christ's Church had this authority.

Arius and his followers did not crawl under a rock after the council ended; they did not give up their heresy and accept the Church's declarations. Rather, he and the bishops who supported him continued with all their might to promulgate their false teachings and gain power within the Church and in the Roman Empire. And they succeeded to a large degree, for a time. Their heresy became so widespread that new Christian converts in areas where the Arians dominated became indoctrinated into their heretical ideas. It took hundreds of years before the heresy was finally eliminated. But the Arian heresy was always just that—a heresy. And those who persisted in it had caused a schism.

More ecumenical councils soon followed. The second one occurred in 381 at Constantinople and declared the teachings of Macedonius, which denied the divinity of the Holy Spirit, to be heretical. The council proclaimed dogmatically that the Holy Spirit is divine and one in being with the Father and with the Son. Ecumenical councils continued to be convened, and there were a total of eight of them prior to the Eastern Orthodox schism in 1054. From then up through the present day, the Orthodox Churches have held no ecumenical councils, nor have any Protestant communities; however, the Catholic Church has continued holding them as necessary.

We have seen that the bishops of Christ's Church, under the pope (who appears in person or through legates), have met in ecumenical councils when a pressing matter of faith must be dealt with and decided upon. What is truth and what is heresy is discerned in these councils, and often, binding decisions are made by them.

How many of these ecumenical councils do Protestants believe to be authoritative? Varying answers are given depending upon the particular Protestant community, but few Protestants would accept more than the first seven ecumenical councils as authoritative in any way, and most accept only selected decrees from the first four.

The important question to ask is, "at what point did the councils stop being authoritative?" Why did God design His Church such that, for over 700 years, ecumenical councils were a primary way in which vitally important matters of the faith were discerned and authoritatively proclaimed but then *remove* His authority from them such that they could no longer be trustworthy?

To a Catholic, a council is valid if it receives the approval of the bishop of Rome, the successor of Peter, to whom Christ gave the "keys to the kingdom of heaven" as well as the authority to bind and loose (see Matt. 16:18–19). The deference given to the bishop of Rome, the pope, by the other patriarchs when these first councils were held is widespread and well documented. For instance, leading up to the Council of Chalcedon in 451—which established Christ as both fully God and fully human—Flavian, the patriarch of Constantinople, wrote the pope about the extremity of the current religious-political conflict and called for his intervention:

> When I began to appeal to the throne of the Apostolic
> See of Peter, the Prince of the Apostles, and to the whole
> sacred synod, which is obedient to Your Holiness, at
> once a crowd of soldiers surrounded me and barred my
> way when I wished to take refuge at the holy al-
> tar....Therefore, I beseech Your Holiness not to permit
> these things to be treated with indifference...but to rise
> up first on behalf of the cause of our orthodox Faith,
> now destroyed by unlawful acts....Further to issue an au-
> thoritative instruction...so that a like faith may every-
> where be preached by the assembly of a united synod of
> fathers, both Eastern and Western. Thus the laws of the
> fathers may prevail and all that has been done amiss be
> rendered null and void. Bring healing to this ghastly
> wound.[2]

This evidence for deference to the pope by brother bishops in the early centuries of the Church could be reproduced many times over.

If Protestantism is true, then God gave the Church authority to make binding decisions about what is truth and what is heresy for over 700 years, and all Christians accepted these decisions as authoritative. But then, inexplicably, God disallowed the Church to hold any further authoritative councils. The Church that Christ built was thus left in a state where she could not make binding declarations on truth and heresy, and she remains so to this day.

The Papacy

Perhaps no office is as well-known or as controversial as that of the papacy. The pope is universally recognized around the world, and depending on whose opinion you ask, he is either admired or scorned. Among the hundreds of men who have held the office since Christ established His Church, there have certainly been several to provide fodder for the cannon of public opinion against the papacy. Many more have served with holiness and humility, to God's glory and the strengthening of His Church.

Regardless of anyone's opinion of the pope or the papacy in general, the historical fact is that the Church has had a pope since the beginning of its existence. Only the most antihistorical fundamentalist Protestants deny that there has been a bishop of Rome from at least the early second century. In fact, we know the names and approximate dates of all of the popes, even from the first century: Peter first, then Linus, Titus, Cletus, and Clement I.

The historical fact of the papacy throughout every Christian century, including the very first ones, makes a compelling case that it was intended to be a perpetual office within the institution that Christ built. The Pope presided over or sent his legates to ecumenical councils and confirmed (or refused confirmation) of their decisions, and members of the Church accepted these decrees as binding.

The Protestant Reformers admired Augustine, perhaps above any other early Christian, and used his voluminous writings to inform their own theological ideas. Yet they did so selectively, for Augustine was a great defender of the authority of the bishop of Rome and his successors, as he demonstrates in this passage against the Donatist heretics:

> You know what the Catholic Church is, and what that is cut off from the Vine; if there are any among you cautious, let them come; let them find life in the Root. Come, brethren, if you wish to be engrafted in the Vine: a grief it is when we see you lying thus cut off. Number the Bishops even from the very seat of Peter: and see every succession in that line of Fathers: that is the Rock against which the proud Gates of Hell prevail not [Matt. 16:18].[3]

If Protestantism is true, then after 1,500 years of having a bishop of Rome, called the prince of the Apostles, the successor of Peter to whom Christ gave the keys to the kingdom of heaven, the office of the papacy was eradicated by God. No longer would His Church have a leader, a "servant of the servants of God."[4] Instead, God left His Church to follow whatever leaders declared themselves to be so in whatever "churches" they founded on the basis of their own personal revelations.

Divine Authority

We know from history, the Bible, and Tradition that Christ established a Church, visible and hierarchically organized, and to which He gave His divine authority. In Luke's Gospel, Jesus says to His disciples: "Whoever listens to you listens to me. Whoever rejects you rejects me. And whoever rejects me rejects the one who sent me" (Luke 10:16). Notice the direct line of authority: the Father sends the Son, and the Son in turn sends the Apostles with His authority, such that listening to them and the men they in turn authorize is equivalent to listening to Jesus and thus also to the Father.

In Matthew's Gospel, we hear that "he called to him his twelve Apostles and gave them authority over unclean spirits, to cast them out, and to heal every disease and every infirmity....'Heal the sick, raise the dead, cleanse lepers, cast out demons' " (Matt. 10:1,8). Finally, in the Gospel according to John, Jesus gives the Apostles divine authority to forgive sins in God's name: "And when he had said this, he breathed on them, and said to them, 'Receive the Holy Spirit. If you forgive the sins of any, they are forgiven; if you retain the sins of any, they are retained' " (John 20:22–23).

Christ later shows He meant what He said when He knocks Saul (who later becomes Paul) off his horse:

> Now Saul, still breathing murderous threats against the
> disciples of the Lord, went to the high priest and asked
> him for letters to the synagogues in Damascus, that, if he
> should find any men or women who belonged to the
> Way, he might bring them back to Jerusalem in chains.
> On his journey, as he was nearing Damascus, a light
> from the sky suddenly flashed around him. He fell to the
> ground and heard a voice saying to him, "Saul, Saul, why
> are you persecuting me?" He said, "Who are you, sir?"
> The reply came, "I am Jesus, whom you are persecuting"
> (Acts 9:1–5).

Notice that Jesus didn't say, "Saul, why are you persecuting *my followers*" but rather, "Why are you persecuting *me*?" For in murdering the leaders of Christ's Church, Saul was rejecting not only them but Christ Himself.

From history, we see the Apostles and then their successors, the bishops, exercising this authority in the Church and the Church thriving under their divinely authorized leadership, even in the midst of horrific persecutions. From the Bible and from Tradition, we understand that the authority Christ gave to the Apostles as the leaders of the Church was transmitted to their successors. It was not intended to be lost when the Apostles died in the first century. Similarly, the promises that Christ made to the Church were understood as permanent; nowhere did Jesus say that at some point He would abandon His Church to let the gates of Hell prevail against her or that the authority He had given her leaders would be revoked.

In spite of these promises, Protestants believe that this visible Church did in fact *lose* God's authority at some point in time, that Christ revoked it when corruption entered into her teachings. Many fundamentalist Protestants believe that the date when the Church became corrupted and lost God's divine authorization was the year 313 when Emperor Constantine ended the persecution of Christians in the empire (the Edict of Milan).

Protestants in general are usually not so exact and instead claim that corruption entered into the Church somewhere between 325 and 600. This claim differs from that of the Mormons (Latter Day Saints) only in the specific date given, for Mormons believe that the Church lost the authority Christ gave her sometime around 70 or 100 (either at the death of Peter or of the last Apostle, which would be John). At that time, they assert, the "Great Apostasy" began, which lasted for around 1,700 years before Christ *reestablished* His authority in the Mormon Church through Joseph Smith in the nineteenth century.

Does the Mormon claim seem plausible? The Word became flesh, and He lived on earth for over thirty years, giving His life for the salvation of all. Then, Christ gave us the Holy Spirit, the spirit "of power, of love, and of self-control" (2 Tim. 1:7), whom He promised would lead the Apostles (and thus the Church) into all truth (see John 16:13). But the Mormon assertion means that the Holy Spirit *utterly failed* to lead the Church into all truth. Indeed, as soon as the last Apostle died, the Church went belly-up for over 1,700 years! The gates of Hell prevailed against the Church and overcame her. Christ failed to keep His Church together and protected from adulterated teachings for even one generation beyond His life on earth. This key claim of Mormonism is not credible, yet the Protestant corollary is substantially similar, only differing in the number of years it took for corruption to taint the Church and her teachings.

Even as a Baptist, I rejected the Mormon claim of the Church losing her authority at the death of the Apostles, but as I pondered this question, I realized that my Protestant beliefs were not so very different. When did *I*, as a Baptist, think that corruption had entered into the Church's teachings (because I certainly did believe that it had)? The truth was that I had never given it that much thought. "It happened in the first four or five centuries perhaps," I mused vaguely. And like most Protestants, I thought that the Reformers had more or less corrected the corrupted teachings and set things right again. What did I think had happened to the Church for the 1,000 years between the corruption and the Reformation? To be honest, I didn't really think about it—nor do most Protestants.

Since Christ established a visible Church in the first century and gave her rightful authority, the burden of proof falls on Protestants to demonstrate that He revoked this authority universally from the Church at some point in time. What event occurred that caused Christ to take away His authority, and which Church leaders were involved in it? Where is the historical evidence for the claim?

These questions are vitally important to have answered, since Protestants most certainly believe that Christ established the Church. But then this Church became corrupted and is what we know today as the Catholic Church, leaving the real Church as the invisible set of believers who did not abandon the gospel in spite of the Catholic Church's heresies.

A Protestant might object, as I once did, that because the Church is purely invisible and spiritual, rather than a visible entity with divinely authorized leaders, the promises Christ made still apply to all the "true believers" in the world, who make up the invisible Church, and though the original, pure Church that Christ founded succumbed to corruption, the *real* Church quietly continued throughout all of the apostate centuries until the Reformation brought them closer again to original biblical doctrines.

The problem with this objection is that Christ definitely founded a visible Church, and the members of His Church were unified together as His mystical Body, of which He is the head.[5] A body is both visible and alive; if you found a severed hand, a foot, an arm, and a toe on the ground, you would not say, "Here is a body" but rather "Here are parts that were severed from a body." Similarly, Christ's mystical Body, the Church, is a visible unity, and when we examine history (as we will in even more detail in subsequent chapters), we see that this Church acted with Christ's authority and that those members who persisted in teaching false doctrines (not those who simply entertained them) were excommunicated as heretics, whereupon they broke away from the Church and caused schisms.

We see the visibility of the Church in what Vincent of Lerins said in the year 434: "What then will a Catholic Christian do if a small portion of the Church has cut itself off from the communion of the universal faith? What, surely, but prefer the soundness of the whole body to the unsoundness of a pestilent and corrupt member."[6] The idea that the Church at some point changed from being visible and united to purely invisible and divided (but still the Church) is an invention of Protestantism in the 1500s. (It should be noted that the Orthodox Churches also reject this novel Protestant claim.)

If Protestantism is true, then either Christ revoked the authority He had given His Church *or* she changed in her essentials from being a unified, visible, and hierarchically organized Body to an invisible and purely spiritual one, merely made up of believers who are embodied. In the latter case, it becomes impossible to know to whom God has given the rightful authority to lead the Church. In Protestantism, there is no Church that can be pointed to as "the Church" but only individual believers, some of whom claim authority because they say that they teach the truth.

The Four Marks of the Church

Stemming directly from the promises made by Christ to His Church, the four marks of the Church are found in the Nicene Creed: "We believe in one, holy, catholic, and apostolic Church."

The first mark, that the Church is *one*, means that she is visibly unified as the Body of Christ. Your body is a visible unity and more than just a mere collection of parts stuck together. Christ's Body is also unified, and the Church is His mystical Body, so she is a unified and visible institution. The Protestant conception of this mark, however, declares that she is *one* only in the sense that the collection of Christians who make up the invisible Church all form one group. In this way, it is not a unified Body but a collection of disconnected body parts (though Protestants do look ahead to a future unification of the Body upon Christ's return).

The second mark, that the Church is *holy*, means that the Church is truly made holy by Christ, the Bridegroom of the Church, by the power of the Holy Spirit. The Catholic Church teaches that Christians truly become holy by God giving them grace, which is divine life, by way of the sacraments (baptism, confirmation, the Eucharist, confession, and so on). The Catholic understanding of holiness is not just that the Christian is "declared holy" by God even though he really isn't but that Christ *infuses* His righteousness into him, transforming him and truly making him holy.

The Protestant teaching on grace is that it is divine aid but not divine life. Holiness comes from Christ *imputing* His righteousness to the Christian and so the Father legally *declares* him to be holy, but in reality he is not transformed into holiness. This Protestant understanding of grace and holiness for the individual Christian is then applied to the Church in general.

The third mark, that the Church is *catholic*, speaks of her universality, as the Catechism of the Catholic Church explains:

> The word "catholic" means "universal," in the sense of "according to the totality" or "in keeping with the whole." The Church is catholic in a double sense: first, the Church is catholic because Christ is present in her. "Where there is Christ Jesus, there is the Catholic

Church." In her subsists the fullness of Christ's body united with its head; this implies that she receives from him "the fullness of the means of salvation" which he has willed: correct and complete confession of faith, full sacramental life, and ordained ministry in apostolic succession. The Church was, in this fundamental sense, catholic on the day of Pentecost and will always be so until the day of the Parousia.[7]

Protestant communities do not claim to be catholic in the above sense; rather, when they recite this part of the creed, the idea they apply is that the invisible Church is catholic in that it encompasses all believers, no matter where they are. No Protestant community claims to have "the fullness of the means of salvation" nor a "correct and complete confession of faith"—the confessions they may ascribe to are useful or authoritative insofar as they square with that community's interpretation of the Bible (or in some cases, a leader's private revelation). Further, Apostolic Succession is rejected, thus catholicity in the sense of being organically connected through time to the Apostles does not exist. Finally, most Protestants believe that the Church was corrupted in her teachings sometime between the second and seventh centuries, demonstrating a lack of catholicity of the Church for at least one thousand years, fully half of the Church's existence in history!

The fourth mark, that the Church is *apostolic*, indicates that the Church is built on the foundation of the Apostles, with Christ as the cornerstone: "So then you are no longer strangers and sojourners, but you are fellow citizens with the holy ones and members of the household of God, built upon the foundation of the Apostles and prophets, with Christ Jesus himself as the capstone" (Eph. 2:19–20). (The "household of God" is the Church: see Heb. 3:4–6.) The Catholic Church teaches that Apostolic Succession is the means by which God transmitted authority from the Apostles to their successors, the bishops, through the laying on of hands—and then in turn to their successors (see 1 Tim. 4:14). These bishops, in communion with the bishop of Rome, the pope, are the divinely authorized leaders of Christ's Church.

We hear this as early as the second century from Irenaeus, bishop of Lyons:

Wherefore it is incumbent to obey the presbyters who are in the Church—those who, as I have shown, possess the succession from the apostles; those who, together with the succession of the episcopate, have received the certain gift of truth, according to the good pleasure of the Father. But [it is also incumbent] to hold in suspicion others who depart from the primitive succession, and assemble themselves together in any place whatsoever, [looking upon them] either as heretics of perverse minds, or as schismatics puffed up and self-pleasing, or again as hypocrites, acting thus for the sake of lucre and vainglory. For all these have fallen from the truth. And the heretics, indeed, who bring strange fire to the altar of God—namely, strange doctrines—shall be burned up by the fire from heaven....But such as rise up in opposition to the truth, and exhort others against the Church of God, [shall] remain among those in hell (*apud inferos*), being swallowed up by an earthquake, even as those who were with Chore, Dathan, and Abiron (Numbers 16:33). But those who cleave asunder, and separate the unity of the Church, [shall] receive from God the same punishment as Jeroboam did.[8]

Protestant communities claim to be apostolic in that they teach the same truth that God gave to the Apostles in the first century. In actuality, they are simply claiming that their community's interpretation of the Bible is God's truth. They then claim that this understanding of apostolicity replaces Apostolic Succession as the means of determining the rightful authority within the church. However, in order for a community's teachings to be compared to truth, truth itself must first be defined. This immediately raises the question of who, exactly, has the authority to *interpret* the Bible and declare what "God's truth" is. This topic will be explored more deeply in subsequent chapters.

The Protestant conception of the four marks of the Church demonstrates how easily we can rationalize away inconsistencies between our beliefs and historical evidence by creating new definitions for phrases. The Nicene Creed is ancient, dating from 325. Protestantism, coming 1,200 years later, affirmed the creed as true, but it fundamentally modified its meaning, including the four marks of the Church.

Celibacy for the Kingdom

It might seem surprising that priestly celibacy and nuns' consecrated virginity for the sake of the Kingdom could possibly be considered a reason *in favor* of the Catholic Church. After all, in the United States and in some other countries in recent times, the scandal of priestly sexual abuse seems to provide an obvious objection to celibacy. In addition, all Protestant communities have categorically rejected celibacy as a required discipline for their clergy or pastors. Consecrated religious sisters have likewise almost entirely vanished from Protestantism.

So what is the basis for Catholicism's teachings on celibacy? It turns out they come straight from Jesus and Paul in the Bible. We hear Jesus address this question in Matthew's Gospel:

> And Pharisees came up to him and tested him by asking, "Is it lawful to divorce one's wife for any cause?" He answered, "Have you not read that he who made them from the beginning made them male and female, and said, 'For this reason a man shall leave his father and mother and be joined to his wife, and the two shall become one flesh'? So they are no longer two but one flesh. What therefore God has joined together, let not man put asunder."
>
> They said to him, "Why then did Moses command one to give a certificate of divorce, and to put her away?" He said to them, "For your hardness of heart Moses allowed you to divorce your wives, but from the beginning it was not so. And I say to you: whoever divorces his wife, except for unchastity, and marries another, commits adultery." The disciples said to him, "If such is the case of a man with his wife, it is not expedient to marry." But he said to them, "Not all men can receive this saying, but only those to whom it is given. For there are eunuchs who have been so from birth, and there are eunuchs who have been made eunuchs by men, and there are eunuchs

who have made themselves eunuchs for the sake of the
kingdom of heaven. He who is able to receive this, let
him receive it" [Matt. 19:1–12].

If this passage's meaning seems unclear to us today, we can look
to what the early Christians taught about this part of Matthew 19.
Gregory Nazianzen wrote,

> Marriage is honourable; but I cannot say that it is more
> lofty than virginity; for virginity were no great thing if it
> were not better than a good thing....A mother she is not,
> but a Bride of Christ she is. The visible beauty is not
> hidden, but that which is unseen is visible to God. All
> the glory of the King's Daughter is within, clothed with
> golden fringes, embroidered whether by actions or by
> contemplation. And she who is under the yoke [of mar-
> riage], let her also in some degree be Christ's; and the
> virgin altogether Christ's. Let the one be not entirely
> chained to the world (Luke 8:14), and let the other not
> belong to the world at all....Have you chosen the life of
> Angels?[9]

Such passages from the writings of the Church Fathers could be
reproduced many times over. While it is true that nowhere is it explicitly commanded that all priests be celibate (and in the Catholic
Church there are many married priests), there exists compelling testimony to know how this passage has always been understood by
Christians. Virginity for the Kingdom is commended, and from early on in the Church we see women and men who consecrated
themselves to God for the sake of the Kingdom as nuns and
priests.

Paul was celibate as far as we know and commends virginity for
the sake of the Kingdom in 1 Corinthians 7:

> I wish that all men were as I am. But each man has his
> own gift from God; one has this gift, another has that.
> Now to the unmarried and the widows I say: It is good
> for them to stay unmarried, as I am. An unmarried man
> is concerned about the Lord's affairs—how he can please
> the Lord. But a married man is concerned about the af-

fairs of this world—how he can please his wife—and his interests are divided. An unmarried woman or virgin is concerned about the Lord's affairs: Her aim is to be devoted to the Lord in both body and spirit. But a married woman is concerned about the affairs of this world— how she can please her husband (1 Cor. 7:7–8,32–34, NIV).

To answer the charge that a priest's infidelity to his vows is a consequence of celibacy and therefore a condemnation of this practice, consider whether men who are unfaithful to their wives are a condemnation of Jesus's teaching on fidelity in marriage? Of course not. Just because a man is not faithful to his vows—whether made to the Church or to his wife—does not mean that the teaching of Christ about fidelity is false but rather that men can fall to temptation and break their vows. Not all are called to celibacy for the Kingdom; most are called to marriage. However, men enter the priesthood and women enter consecrated life with eyes wide open, living many years in community before making their final vows of poverty, chastity, and obedience. They can leave at any time if they discern they are called to marriage instead. It is a choice of vocation that God gives us to discern freely, and both vocations are beautiful.

With this biblical and historical support, why did Protestants abandon the discipline of celibacy? The magisterial reformer Martin Luther rejected priestly celibacy in a reaction against the Church's distinction between clergy and laity. (The Church taught that clergy were given a special mark by God in the sacrament of holy orders.) Anglican historian Alister McGrath explains this well:

> [Luther believed that the Church] is fundamentally a gathering of believers, not a divinely ordained institution with sacred powers and authority vested exclusively in its clergy. All believers, men and women, by virtue of their baptism, are priests. Luther noted an important corollary to this doctrine: the clergy should be free to marry, like all other Christians. This right to clerical marriage rapidly became a defining characteristic of Protestantism.[10]

Protestants' rejection of celibacy for the Kingdom comes then, not from the Bible, which commends the practice in the words of Christ Himself, but from following a tradition begun by Martin Luther in his reaction against some abuses of clerical power.

If Protestantism is true, then Jesus established celibacy for the Kingdom, Paul affirmed it both in his own life and as an exhortation for all called to it, and the Holy Spirit made this vocation within the Church fruitful for centuries, but then in the 1500s it was right to abandon the practice.

Beneficial Requirements

Following up on this teaching of celibacy for the Kingdom, one of the arguments against it is that it ought to be optional. If a priest wants to marry, great. But if he wants to "renounce marriage for the sake of the kingdom," he can do that, too. Further, "Why make going to church once per week a requirement? Wouldn't it be more respectful of peoples' freedom to make it optional so that they only go when they feel led by the Spirit to go or want to go for love of God, rather than compelling them to go for fear of hell due to committing a grave sin?"

The short answer is, the Church wants her members to draw closer and closer to Christ in their life on earth, that they may enjoy life forever in Heaven with God. The Church also knows human nature and man's tendency toward sin ("concupiscence"), and so she mandates for the good of the person's soul that at a minimum he spend at least one out of the 168 hours during the week with God in the communal act of worship. Protestant communities have removed this obligation. I have many friends who are faithful Protestant Christians who do not go to church even once per month. (They jokingly tell me on days they miss that they went to "Bedside Baptist.") Why don't they go every week? "We are busy; it's a pain to get all the children loaded up; I didn't wake up in time; I haven't found a good church home yet; I am not getting anything out of going to church; I can just worship God on my own, in my home, in nature," etc.

I understand. There are many times when I would rather not go to Mass on Sunday. But I know that the Church, with Christ's wisdom, has mandated it for my salvation. I go to Mass and worship God in the liturgy with my brothers and sisters. I receive our Lord Jesus Christ in the Holy Eucharist and am strengthened against mortal sin. My sins are forgiven by Him, and I listen to His Word, as well as a homily delving more deeply into the mysteries of our Faith.

Priestly celibacy fits into this explanation, too. Most of us have strong sexual desires. God knows this fact; after all, it's the way he made us. So He calls only certain people to renounce marriage for the sake of the Kingdom by living celibately, as a sign of the reality of the Resurrection, when "they neither marry nor are given in marriage, but are like the angels in heaven" (Matt. 22:30). Even people he calls to this life have sexual desires, and given the option, due to our concupiscence, many might decide at some point to exercise the option and get married, back-pedaling from their promise to renounce marriage for the sake of the Kingdom. Thus, making priestly celibacy a requirement helps those called to this vocation remain faithful to their vows to God. Paul commends this life; Jesus lived it, and many in every generation since have followed their examples.

If Protestantism is true, then almost nothing is binding upon us as Christians besides personal faith. Protestant pastors may fear obligating anyone to even come to the Sunday service, because members of their church can easily reject any admonition and leave for another Protestant church that doesn't make such requirements. It is true that the greatest motivation for Christian action is love, first of God and then of neighbor, and it is true that people should never be coerced or forced to be involved in church. Still, we who believe in God and in His Son cannot just have a personal faith that we never share with the community. Nor is it good for us to hide our God-given talents under a rock. Christ commanded that we celebrate the Eucharist, and He commanded us to be baptized and to obey His teachings. So there is a very real obligation to follow Him within a faith community.

The Saints

As a Protestant, I once called the saints "the Catholic Hall of Fame members" when talking about them with a Catholic friend of mine. While that is true in a lighthearted sense, it doesn't do justice to the saints, through whom the glory of God has shined most brightly.

When I, as a Protestant, started reading the lives of the saints, I felt cheated: "Why haven't I been told about all these amazingly faithful people?" Their books didn't show up *anywhere* in the Christian bookstores I went to, nor very often in the secular bookstores. I had read most of the "Left Behind" series but nothing by Augustine, Thomas Aquinas, Athanasius, or Francis de Sales. Something was wrong about that. The spectrum of my Evangelical Protestant reading began with the Bible and then skipped eighteen centuries to modern Christian works, even though doctrines stemming from both the first centuries of the Church and also ones from the sixteenth century Reformers were part of my beliefs.

Protestants thus miss out on learning about the great men and women who lived in the so-called "Dark Ages," Christians to whom we owe a debt of gratitude for preserving the Faith through these centuries. God did not "check out" during this time period; nor did He abandon His Bride; nor did He quit leading Christians to take the gospel to the ends of the earth and to reform the Church in their own countries. Rather, this era was like every other in the history of the Church and the world; there were weeds and wheat growing up together—sinners who became saints and unrepentant sinners who opposed God and His Church.

Those the Church calls saints were men and women who loved God and who accepted His love in a way that penetrated every part of them. As a questioning Protestant, I longed to love God as they did. They were special; they were the very best that Christians could be, the fulfillment of Christ's commands to love God and one another with all our hearts. And all of these people were unabashedly *Catholic*. They were as Catholic as the pope, believing in the real presence of Jesus Christ in the Eucharist, in the power of confession, in celibacy for the Kingdom, in the authority of the Church, and in the Holy Spirit's guidance of her. Modern-day saints like Mother Teresa of Calcutta give us a glimpse as to what the great saints of history must have been like: permeated with Christ's transforming love and mercy, tireless in their service to those most in need, supremely hopeful for the salvation of every person in the world.

If Protestantism is true, then all of the saints from the fourth century to the sixteenth believed in an adulterated gospel taught by a heretical Church. And though they may have loved God, they did so while promulgating erroneous, perhaps even evil, teachings on important matters of the Faith. While some of their piety and actions are to be commended, they cannot be looked to as reliable forefathers in the Faith because of their errors and support of a Church which had become corrupted to the core. If they had only followed the Bible, they could have corrected the errors of the Church as the later Reformers did. But God, quite strangely, allowed even the humblest and most faithful men and women over these many centuries to go astray and lead others astray in their beliefs about God, the nature of the Church, the sacraments, and countless other matters. So sadly, the lessons of much of their lives—and deaths—are worth little to our spiritual walks today.

Chapter Four
Reformation: Schism or Branches?

Nathon and his wife, Michelle, grew up in solid Protestant churches in the Midwest. They became college sweethearts, married, and then moved down to Texas where they began their careers. That's where he and I met. We became acquainted, but it was some time before I knew he was thinking about these important issues separating Catholics and Protestants.

He and his wife were attending a newly-formed community that spun off from a Southern Baptist church. The congregation's demographic was young and primarily white, and the church services featured a dynamic pastor and contemporary music.

After knowing Nathon for a number of years, he asked if I wanted to go to lunch one day. He was a thoughtful young man, humble but also very intelligent. At lunch, he revealed that he had been reading my blog for a long time and thinking about the issues I posted about. Nathon was wrestling with many of these issues and wanted someone to talk to more about them. He had already questioned his pastor about the canon of Scripture and why they accepted the books of the Protestant Bible, but his pastor unfortunately had never questioned the canon and could not give him a compelling answer.

I learned that some of his family descended from Romanian Orthodox Christians, so he was familiar with the ancient faith of the Orthodox Churches (which are very close to Catholicism in their beliefs and liturgies). In addition, another portion of his family is Catholic (practicing and otherwise). The inconsistent witness to the Catholic Faith given by his relatives has unfortunately not helped the Church's credibility in his mind.

Nathon knows the arguments for the Catholic Church now and intellectually finds some of them solid. He still wrestles with questions on the canon and church authority, and as he continues to pray and research. I'm always ready to discuss these issues with him and offer what help I can for his journey.

The Reformation

The Protestant Reformation was composed of several different movements in the sixteenth century: the German Reformation led by Martin Luther, the Anglican Reformation in England, the Reformed Protestants led by John Calvin, and the Radical Reformation (also called the Anabaptists). Martin Luther is largely responsible for igniting the others, though Ulrich Zwingli in Switzerland also began his reform movement around the same time. (Zwingli influenced several of the nascent Protestant movements but died young.) These movements were not centrally coordinated or in agreement with one another over many issues of the Christian Faith—they often fought against one another bitterly—but they shared a common enemy in the Catholic Church, rejecting many Church doctrines and practices.

At the heart of any Christian's examination of the Reformation must be the ultimate determination as to whether it represented a set of new *branches* in the *tree* of Christianity or whether it was actually a set of *heresies* that caused *schisms* from the Church that Christ established. Protestants of course believe it to be the former, and Catholics the latter. In this chapter we will consider reasons for the Catholic Church from the examination of the Reformation and the Reformers.

Heresy and Schism in History

Recall that Paul admonished the church in Corinth to remain in unity: "Now I beseech you, brethren, by the name of our Lord Jesus Christ, that you all speak the same thing, and that there be no schisms among you" (1 Cor. 1:10, Douay-Rheims). The early Christians were also adamant against schisms, as Irenaeus, bishop of Lyons, wrote in the second century:

> [The spiritual man] shall also judge those who give rise to schisms, who are destitute of the love of God, and who look to their own special advantage rather than to the unity of the Church; and who for trifling reasons, or any kind of reason which occurs to them, cut in pieces and

divide the great and glorious body of Christ, and so far as in them lies, destroy it—men who prate of peace while they give rise to war, and do in truth strain out a gnat, but swallow a camel. For they can bring about no "reformation" of enough importance to compensate for the evil arising from their schism....True knowledge is that which consists in the doctrine of the apostles, and the ancient constitution of the Church throughout all the world, and the distinctive manifestation of the body of Christ according to the successions of the bishops, by which they have handed down that Church which exists in every place.[1]

Early on in the Church, movements arose that taught doctrines contrary to the teachings of Christ to the Apostles (preserved in both the sacred Scriptures and the apostolic Tradition). One of the first of these was a group of Judaizers known as the Ebionites; they arose in the early 100s and denied the divinity of Christ as well as the virgin birth. Christ to them was a wise teacher, but not God. The Church, entrusted by the Apostles with the truth of the Faith, declared these beliefs heretical. John, the last of the Apostles to die, had only passed away a few years prior to this time. The Ebionites were not a new branch of the tree of Christianity; they were a heretical schism from the Church.

By what authority did the Church discern and then declare that certain movements were heretical, movements which were often led by clergy within the Church herself? Irenaeus tells us:

Since, however, it would be very tedious, in such a volume as this, to reckon up the successions of all the Churches, we do put to confusion all those who, in whatever manner, whether by an evil self-pleasing, by vainglory, or by blindness and perverse opinion, assemble in unauthorized meetings; [we do this] by indicating that tradition derived from the apostles, of the very great, the very ancient, and universally known Church founded and organized at Rome by the two most glorious apostles, Peter and Paul; as also [by pointing out] the faith preached to men, which comes down to our time by means of the successions of the bishops. For it is a mat-

> ter of necessity that every Church should agree with this
> Church, on account of its preeminent authority, that is,
> the faithful everywhere, inasmuch as the tradition has
> been preserved continuously by those [faithful] who exist
> everywhere.[2]

Christ, then, had given the Church the deposit of faith in the apostolic Tradition ("tradition derived from the Apostles"), contained in both written and unwritten forms. And this Tradition was preserved by the authorized churches who were led by the bishops in direct succession from the Apostles and in union with the Church of Rome, founded by Peter and Paul. *This* was the visible Church, the one built by Christ and given divine authority and guidance to discern truth and detect heresy. Between the second and fifteenth centuries, many other heresies arose, and for each one, the Church discerned whether the doctrines being proposed were true or false.

Martin Luther was a German priest and theology professor who lived from the late fifteenth to the mid-sixteenth century. He sparked the Protestant Reformation in 1517 with his seemingly innocuous posting of a protest against various Church practices and teachings, including the sale of indulgences—this practice was not a doctrine of the Church, but the Church had (imprudently) used it to raise money, and now it was being abused by greedy clergy. Luther had also developed other controversial ideas, ones which did run counter to the Church's teachings, and he began to propose these ideas as well. He engaged his fellow priests in debate, and his teachings grew in popularity in large part because the sociopolitical climate of the time in Germany was ripe for an upheaval of the current order, which included Christ's Church.

At the beginning of his outcry, even until the Diet of Worms[3] in 1521, "Luther had no intention of breaking away from the church. Nothing, he commented, could be achieved through schism. His hope was to reform the church from within....Yet his excommunication by Leo X in 1520 and his open condemnation by the Edict of Worms the following year seemed to rule out any such possibility."[4] Like Arius[5] before him, Luther responded to excommunication by rejecting the Church's authority and continuing to teach his own opinions as divine truth. He could have chosen at that point to take time to humbly reflect on his theology and the Church's guidance, but unfortunately he did not do so. He could have chosen to continue to work for reform within the Church while being careful not to elevate his every opinion to the level of divine truth. But instead, the sad result was a heretical schism from the Church that Christ established—a Church that was surely in need of reform and renewal, which should have been attempted and accomplished from *within* the Church and not by bitter division.

The tragic thing is that some of Luther's objections were justified; he exposed grave abuses that many of the clergy were engaging in at the time. And he was even right in correcting one erroneous teaching of the local church in his part of Germany (a false teaching that ran contrary to the actual doctrine of the Catholic Church, something Luther perhaps did not realize, given late-medieval communication limitations). The Protestant Reformation, while objectively unjustified as a schism, was not a baseless rebellion against a Church full of ardently faithful Christians; rather, members of the Catholic Church, including even certain popes and bishops, provided plenty of reasons for a faithful person to protest and demand reform. Luther made the mistake, however, of thinking that all of his theological opinions must be right, so instead of championing reform within the Church and humbly accepting some needed correction, Luther stiffened his neck, broke his vows, and refused to submit to any authority save that of himself.

If Protestantism is true, then throughout all of the history of the Church until the Reformation, a heresy was a heresy and a schism was a schism, but the schisms caused by the Reformers were instead new branches on a tree, in spite of the fact that they caused divisions from the Church like every other schism in history had done. Martin Luther was well-intentioned and saw true abuses and evil practices by some leaders in the Church, but unlike the great saints before and after him, he decided to disobey the Church and abandoned any attempt to reform her from within. Had he made different choices, we would likely be calling him St. Martin Luther the Reformer—in the true sense of the word.

Mary's Perpetual Virginity and Her Title of "Mother of God"

If you were to ask many Protestants if they would call the Virgin Mary, "the Mother of God," you would receive horrified looks. It is "those Catholics" who give Mary such titles and "worship" her. But Protestants give Mary her biblical due, which is to say, she was the "Mother of Jesus" and no more—certainly "God" has no human parent. Protestants are partly right in their objection, and partly very wrong. Let's examine what the Church means when she says that Mary is the Mother of God:

> In proclaiming Mary "Mother of God," the Church thus intends to affirm that she is the "Mother of the Incarnate Word, who is God." Her motherhood does not, there-fore, extend to all the Trinity, but only to the Second Person, the Son, who, in becoming incarnate, took his human nature from her. Motherhood is a relationship of person to person: a mother is not only mother of the body or of the physical creature born of her womb, but of the person she begets. Thus having given birth, ac-cording to his human nature, to the person of Jesus, who is a divine person, Mary is the Mother of God....Mary's divine motherhood refers only to the human begetting of the Son of God but not, however, to his divine birth. The Son of God was eternally begotten of God the Fa-ther, and is consubstantial with him.[6]

The Church had always believed this teaching, but it did not have to be dogmatically declared until 431 when Nestorius, the Pa-triarch of Constantinople, began to challenge the belief, saying in-stead that Mary could only be called the mother of Christ or the mother of Jesus's "human nature." The problem with this idea is that a mother is a mother of a *person*, not of a *nature*. In the one di-vine *Person* of Jesus Christ, there exist two natures—one human and one divine—in what is called the hypostatic union, so since Mary was Jesus's mother, and Jesus is God, Mary is the Mother of God.

Martin Luther himself affirmed this teaching unreservedly:

> In this work whereby she was made the Mother of God,
> so many and such great good things were given her that
> no one can grasp them....Not only was Mary the mother
> of him who is born [in Bethlehem], but of him who, be-
> fore the world, was eternally born of the Father, from a
> Mother in time and at the same time man and God.[7]

John Calvin, the other great magisterial reformer, also openly supported this title:

> It cannot be denied that God in choosing and destining
> Mary to be the Mother of his Son, granted her the high-
> est honor...Elizabeth called Mary Mother of the Lord,
> because the unity of the person in the two natures of
> Christ was such that she could have said that the mortal
> man engendered in the womb of Mary was at the same
> time the eternal God.[8]

Most Protestants today would balk at agreeing with Luther and Calvin on this doctrine, not realizing that rejecting it leads to serious theological errors, especially to a misunderstanding of who Christ is. This is the danger that the Church's bishops in the fifth century fully realized.

The Reformers belief in Catholic Marian dogmas goes further, however; they also believed in Mary's perpetual virginity! Luther wrote passionately and clearly in defense of this dogma: "Christ, our Savior, was the real and natural fruit of Mary's virginal womb....This was without the cooperation of a man, and she remained a virgin after that."[9] In an intellectual defense of his stance, Luther also wrote,

> Scripture does not say or indicate that she later lost her
> virginity....When Matthew says that Joseph did not know
> Mary carnally until she had brought forth her son, it does
> not follow that he knew her subsequently; on the con-
> trary, it means that he never did know her....This bab-
> ble...is without justification....he [one who interprets the
> Bible against Mary's perpetual virginity] has neither no-
> ticed nor paid any attention to either Scripture or the
> common idiom.[10]

John Calvin also defended the probability of Mary's perpetual virginity, criticizing one of Jerome's opponents in the early centuries of the Church: "Helvidius displayed excessive ignorance in concluding that Mary must have had many sons, because Christ's 'brothers' are sometimes mentioned."[11] Calvin continued:

> The inference [Helvidius] drew from [Matt. 1:25] was, that Mary remained a virgin no longer than till her first birth, and that afterwards she had other children by her husband....No just and well-grounded inference can be drawn from these words...as to what took place after the birth of Christ. He is called "first-born"; but it is for the sole purpose of informing us that he was born of a virgin....What took place afterwards the historian does not inform us....No man will obstinately keep up the argument, except from an extreme fondness for disputation.[12]

A Protestant might object that Luther and Calvin were still too tainted by encrusted Catholic traditions to realize that these Marian doctrines were unbiblical and false. They had been too long immersed in "Romanism" to see the clear biblical truth on these matters.

However, these men had clearly demonstrated little compunction in throwing out doctrine after doctrine held by the Catholic Church, even the most fundamental teachings on the Church's nature, her divine authority, and which books make up the Bible. Therefore it is unlikely that they would have had any scruples in rejecting the Marian dogmas, which to modern-day Protestants seem so obviously false. Instead, we see them defending these teachings using arguments from both faith and reason.

Assuming, then, that these Marian dogmas are false, what does it say that the magisterial Reformers believed in them? If they made such grave errors here in interpreting the Scriptures, how are they to be considered credible with other doctrines? Remember, these were the men responsible for the bedrock Protestant doctrines of *sola fide* (justification by faith alone) and *sola Scriptura* (the Bible alone), yet they saw no contradiction between what was said in the Bible and these Marian dogmas, which largely come from sacred Tradition.

If Protestantism is true, then the men who formulated the great doctrines of the Reformation, upon which all Protestants base their beliefs, erred seriously on many teachings, ones that Protestants today would denounce as completely unbiblical.

Martin Luther's Personal Holiness

Since Protestantism is so strongly based on the views of a single person—many core beliefs directly and indirectly rely on Martin Luther's ideas—that person's personal holiness would hopefully be as great as possible. However, Luther's ugly words about Jewish people must be addressed. In his 1543 treatise, *On the Jews and Their Lies*, Luther wrote that the Jews are "full of the devil's feces...which they wallow in like swine."[13] He wrote many other repugnant things about them, which do not need to be further reproduced. How can it be that Luther had the love of God in his heart when he said such things of his neighbors? Certainly not many of us are completely free of prejudice, but perhaps we *should* strive to be before we endeavor to fix God's Church. How is it possible for a man to have such a blind spot of hatred and yet also have been spiritually commissioned to reform the Church?

It might also come as a shock to Protestants that Luther, claiming *sola Scriptura*, believed a Christian man could marry multiple women (polygamy):

> I confess that I cannot forbid a person to marry several wives, for it does not contradict the Scripture. If a man wishes to marry more than one wife he should be asked whether he is satisfied in his conscience that he may do so in accordance with the word of God. In such a case the civil authority has nothing to do in such a matter.[14]

A Protestant who respects Luther faces a difficult problem when confronting these facts about him, and the best solution seems to be to ignore this dark and ignorant side of his heart. Surely, we offer such grace to normal people on a daily basis. But Luther is not an everyday brother in Christ. He is held up as the virtuous reformer of the corrupt Church, a man extremely faithful to Christ. Yet Christ commanded us to love our neighbor as ourselves and also to remain faithful to a wife as Christ is to His Church. Yet Luther remained shaky on those points. This is the problem with putting too much stock into one person (other than Jesus Christ).

If Protestantism is true, then Martin Luther, the leader of the Reformation and the primary originator of its new doctrines, needed to have been a saintly man, one full of love for God and neighbor, but Luther's writings and actions demonstrate that he was far from these virtues.

The Catholic Perspective on Protestants Today

Many Protestants read the decrees from the Council of Trent, held by the Catholic Church in the mid-1500s, and decide that they must be "heretics" and "anathema" in the eyes of the Church. This is not true. The term anathema was synonymous with "excommunicated," beginning with the Council of Nicaea in 325, where those in the Church who denied Christ's divinity incurred excommunication upon themselves. Anathema later became differentiated to be a formal action of the Church only taken against particularly dangerous and antagonistic heretics, and in 1983, the Church completely did away with the notion. Additionally, almost no Protestants are formal heretics. The Catechism of the Catholic Church defines *formal heresy* thusly: "Heresy is the obstinate post-baptismal denial of some truth which must be believed with divine and catholic faith, or it is likewise an obstinate doubt concerning the same."[15] To be a heretic requires that you first be a baptized Catholic and then that you, obstinately and knowingly, reject dogmas ("truths which must be believed") of the Church (Christ's resurrection; the divinity of Christ, the Holy Spirit, and the Father; the hypostatic union; etc.).

The document from Vatican II that discusses the Catholic Church's understanding of Protestant Christians is the Decree on Ecumenism (*Unitatis Redintegratio*). It answers the question of whether Protestants today bear responsibility for the divisions caused by the Reformation:

> Even in the beginnings of this one and only Church of
> God there arose certain rifts, which the Apostle strongly

condemned. But in subsequent centuries much more serious dissensions made their appearance and quite large
communities came to be separated from full communion
with the Catholic Church—for which, often enough,
men of both sides were to blame. The children who are
born into these Communities and who grow up believing
in Christ cannot be accused of the sin involved in the separation, and the Catholic Church embraces upon them
as brothers, with respect and affection. For men who believe in Christ and have been truly baptized are in communion with the Catholic Church even though this
communion is imperfect.[16]

The children "born into these Communities" include the vast
majority of Protestant Christians alive today: Baptists, Methodists,
Lutherans, churches of Christ, Brethren, all the Pentecostals, etc.
They are *not* culpable for the sin involved in the separation from the
Church. We are all, in a sense, doing the best we can with what we
know.

Let's examine more deeply how the Catholic Church views these
ecclesial communities. For instance, do Protestants have the Holy
Spirit and access to salvation? The Decree on Ecumenism explains:

Moreover, some and even very many of the significant
elements and endowments which together go to build up
and give life to the Church itself, can exist outside the
visible boundaries of the Catholic Church: the written
word of God; the life of grace; faith, hope and charity,
with the other interior gifts of the Holy Spirit, and visible
elements too....It follows that the separated Churches
and Communities as such, though we believe them to be
deficient in some respects, have been by no means deprived of significance and importance in the mystery of
salvation. For the Spirit of Christ has not refrained from
using them as means of salvation which derive their effi-
cacy from the very fullness of grace and truth entrusted
to the Church.[17]

As is evident from these passages, the Catholic Church views the
Orthodox Churches and Protestant communities with great respect

and recognizes that the Holy Spirit, in spite of the disunity, works through them in God's plan of salvation. However, we are still called to unity. That means that each of us, according to the gifts we have been given by God, must seek that unity that Christ called for.

Unlike some Protestant communities who believe Catholics are idol worshippers and the pope the anti-Christ, the Catholic Church calls Protestants brothers—separated, but brothers nonetheless. Through their baptisms, Protestants receive the Holy Spirit and His gifts and fruit, and God in His power and graciousness works through them to bring others to salvation.

A New Reformation Needed?

One day my wife and I drove by a church building in our town and spotted its electronic marquee proclaiming the "Bishop Spong Lecture Series." Bishop John Shelby Spong is a retired Episcopal bishop whom I first encountered in Mark Shea's book, *By What Authority?*, where Spong is described as one of the members of a group called "The Jesus Seminar." The Jesus Seminar is a misnomer, as they should more accurately be called "The Jesus and Bible Deconstructionists." Bishop Spong did his part by publishing several books in which he outlined his denials of such doctrines as the virgin birth and the Resurrection, both of which he claims did not happen as the Bible says they did.

Bishop Spong sees a need for a new Reformation and calls for it with his twelve theses:

> Martin Luther ignited the Reformation of the sixteenth-century by nailing to the door of the church in Wittenberg in 1517 the 95 Theses that he wished to debate....My theses are far smaller in number than were those of Martin Luther, but they are far more threatening theologically. The issues to which I now call the Christians of the world to debate are these:
> 1. Theism, as a way of defining God, is dead. So most theological God-talk is today meaningless. A new way to speak of God must be found.
> 2. Since God can no longer be conceived in theistic terms, it becomes nonsensical to seek to understand Je-

sus as the incarnation of the theistic deity. So the Chris-
tology of the ages is bankrupt.
3. The Biblical story of the perfect and finished creation
from which human beings fell into sin is pre-Darwinian
mythology and post-Darwinian nonsense.
4. The virgin birth, understood as literal biology, makes
Christ's divinity, as traditionally understood, impossible.[18]

The list continues, but I think four items will suffice to give you an
idea of how radical Spong's ideas area.

Bishop Spong likens his actions to those of Martin Luther, but
would Protestants view his "new Reformation" as a new branch on
the Christian tree, a true reformation of a Christianity that has once
again lost its way? Or would they call it a heretical schism? Of
course they would call it the latter. To break from Christ's Church
is never right to do. But that means that when Martin Luther broke
from the Church and led many after him, it was wrong. It means
that Bishop Spong, in calling for a new Reformation (i.e., a new
schism), is wrong. We do not need another schism, nor should we
create yet another church, which only adds to the divisions within
Christianity. What we need is to follow Christ back to the Church
He founded. Either His Church visibly exists and can be found, or
it doesn't. Either it teaches the truth without error, or it doesn't.

A Protestant might object that Bishop Spong's theses are "clearly" false, because they deny the teachings of traditional Christian
orthodoxy and the way that the Bible has been interpreted by the
majority of Christians throughout the ages.

But why is that a problem? Luther's teachings and those of the
Reformation also denied many truths of traditional Christian orthodoxy, yet Protestants believe that the changes in doctrine and the
break from the Catholic Church were both correct and justified.
After all, it is Protestantism that democratized the Church and
made biblical interpretation accessible to all, such that an individual
like Bishop Spong is not bound by any institutional church authority but is free to discover and denounce errors in what Christians
have always believed, based on how he interprets the Bible.

If Protestantism is true, then there is no principled reason why
Spong could not start a new Reformation that would do for the
Christianity of today what Luther's Reformation did for the Church

in the 1500s, since, by Protestant acclaim, Luther and the other Reformers did a noble thing when they broke from the Church to rebuild it from the ground up.

The Need for Reformation in Every Century of the Church

Was there a need for reform in the sixteenth century of Christ's Church? Yes! The Church at the turn of that century had just suffered terribly under the least faithful pope in history, Alexander VI. So why is it wrong that Martin Luther and the Reformers broke from the Church in the Protestant Reformation? It is wrong because the Church is always in need of being reformed from the inside, but the Reformation was a schism that tried to reestablish the Church from the outside. This is an impossible action, since Christ established His Church once for all time at Pentecost after His Resurrection and Ascension.

The history of Christendom is riddled with appalling, stupefying, and even disgusting events. In every century, there have been plenty of good reasons to start a reformation. Priests abused their power; Christians slaughtered pagans and other Christians; priests took concubines after vowing celibacy; bishops bought their ecclesiastical offices; ineffectual and even dissolute popes acted greedily and selfishly. The choice that every dissatisfied Christian has had within Christ's Church since the beginning has been either to schism and start another church, based on a reaction to the proposed evil, or to work for internal reform. The latter option has proven significantly more difficult, but also more worthwhile.

Saints like Francis of Assisi, whom God told to repair His Church, and Catherine of Siena, who boldly admonished the popes to do what was right in God's sight, faced down horrific scandals and heresies in their days, but like Hosea, they responded to the tarnished Bride of Christ by calling her back to her Bridegroom—not sending her away in divorce. Martin Luther, John Calvin, and the other Reformers temporarily succeeded in separating themselves from the particular abuses of the Church during their day, but they also separated themselves from the fullness of the truth and the fullness of the means of salvation that Christ had given to the Church. Babies were thrown out with bath water, and since the

Protestant communities they founded were, like the Catholic Church, full of faulty human beings, inevitably "corruption" entered their communities as well. Running away from problems never solves anything. God calls us to face them head-on.

The saints understood that love for Christ meant that they also must love His Church, cultivating the wheat within her while uprooting the weeds. It is understandable that someone seeing the abuses and evil deeds committed by members of the Church (in any century) would be tempted to reject her altogether as rotten to the core.

Anglican Protestant historian Alister McGrath, however, debunks this caricature of the Church at the time of the Reformation:

> The tidal wave of studies of local archives and private correspondence has confirmed the suspicions of an early generation of scholars—that it is unacceptable to determine the state of the pre-Reformation European church through the eyes of its leading critics, such as Luther and Calvin. It is increasingly clear that attempts to depict the late medieval church as morally and theologically corrupt, unpopular, and in near-terminal decline cannot be sustained on the basis of the evidence available. As in every period, the church possessed strengths and weaknesses and sought to consolidate the former and address the latter. It is now clear that Catholic reforming movements were not a response to the criticisms of the Protestant Reformers but were deeply enmeshed within the pre-Reformation church—where, paradoxically, they created an appetite for reform that laid the ground for Protestantism in some respects.[19]

The desire to purify the Church was not new with Luther. It also appeared in the fourth century in the heresy of Donatism. The Donatists arose in the year 311, around the time Emperor Constantine promulgated the Edict of Milan, which largely ended the persecutions of Christians in the Roman Empire. They were a rigorist group, who in their disgust with those Christians who had renounced their faith under the duress of Roman torture, sought to forbid these repentant men and women from returning to the

Church. They also claimed that any sacraments performed by such Christians were invalid—a dangerous precedent that conditioned the gracious action of God upon the holiness of men.

Their teachings were condemned by Pope Militades, on the basis that Christ's mercy is boundless and never turns away any man who is sincerely repentant, but the Donatists continued to maintain that they were the true Church and persisted in their schism for a full hundred years, until Augustine of Hippo in North Africa definitively ended it. For many years, the missionaries sent by Augustine to convert the Donatists were brutalized, blinded, and even murdered. At the end of the schism in the year 411, in Africa alone, there were around 300 Donatist bishops, approximately equal to the number of orthodox ones.[20] Augustine and Pope Militades showed the way of true reform, countering the Donatists' arrogant desire for divine justice with Christ's boundless mercy. And the Donatist schism was ended by their humility and perserverance.

God called Francis in 1206 while kneeling in prayer in the small, broken-down chapel of San Damiano. Francis heard a voice speak to him from the crucifix: "Francis, go and repair my church, which, as you see, is nearly falling down!"[21] Francis took God's words literally and began physically rebuilding the chapel stone-by-stone. He gathered donations and sold all he had to aid the effort, but he soon realized that God was calling him to reform the *heart* of the Church by following Christ in the radical way of poverty and total trust in God's providence. Men gathered around him, desiring to follow his example, and the Franciscans were born. Today, the Franciscans are found in every continent, serving the poorest of the poor both materially and spiritually, from the ghettos of the inner cities to the war-torn countries in Africa. Francis demonstrated how reform should be done in Christ's Church: from within, with humility, by faithful example, and in obedience to Christ speaking through His Church.

If Protestantism is true, then in the 1500s, for the first time in the history of the Church, a group that left the Church and broke communion with her to form another "Church" was actually following God's will. Additionally, because Protestantism was a decentralized set of movements, the Church was "reformed" by *several* conflicting groups of Christians who contradicted one another on which of the old doctrines were false and which were true. The mystical Body of Christ, which is a unity, became a disunity in defiance of Christ's prayer in John 17, but somehow that disunity was willed by Christ instead of being what it always had been in the past: a heretical schism from the Church.

Chapter Five
The Canon of Scripture

Tom and I first "met" over internet blogs. He started his blog as a forum to think through issues presented to him by a Catholic co-worker, particularly focusing on whether any church taught the fullness of the truth. I found his blog early on and contributed comments whenever I could to demonstrate the reasonableness of the Catholic Church.

A few years passed, and Tom's blog became popular. As he honed in on the issue of authority dividing Catholics and Protestants, his posts began drawing many comments from both sides. He continued to discern where God's truth in its fullness could be found. At home, he faced tension over his exploration, because his wife was not feeling drawn even to investigate the Catholic Church's claims. She was concerned that Tom would even consider becoming Catholic. To his credit, Tom moved very methodically in his study of Catholicism, leaving no stone unturned, knowing that he was responsible for the spiritual leadership of his wife and sons.

As this was unfolding, my wife and I were making a trip to the East coast and providentially were able to meet with Tom and his family. We only had an hour to chat, but it was great to connect in person after having traded blog comments and emails for so long. I learned that he was being trained as a military lawyer, which accounted for his penetrating questions about authority and other differences between Catholics and Protestants.

A short while later, Tom and a group of Catholic converts who came from the Reformed Protestant faith, started a group blog together. Tom wrote with credibility as one who was still a Protestant, looking for answers to the toughest questions. Specifically, he focused on the canon of Scripture, laying out the Catholic argument for the canon and pointing out Protestantism's inability to articulate its canon while also remaining consistent with its other principles.

Back at home, he and his wife prayed and studied together. She followed her husband's lead in searching for the truth, even though at first she personally did not want to do so. Amazingly, after several years, Tom and his wife announced that they and their children would be entering into full communion with the Catholic Church. The canon of Scripture had been the keystone, but many other arguments and evidence had built up in his mind an unassailable case for the Church.

The Centrality of the Canon

No issue is more central to the Catholic-Protestant discussion than the canon of Scripture. Ultimately every difference between Catholics and Protestants comes down to authority, and since Protestantism teaches the doctrine of *sola Scriptura*, that the Bible alone is the ultimate authority, knowing which books make up the Bible is absolutely critical. One would think that this issue would be an open-and-shut case, but as we will see, it is anything but that—which makes it a crucible for arguments from both sides about authority.

The canon of Scripture is the list of books that make up the Bible. In other words, it's Bible's "table of contents." Protestants have sixty-six books in their Bible and Catholics have seventy-three. Both of us can't be right. It stands to reason that the only books that should be included in the Christian Bible are those God Himself has inspired (or "breathed," see 2 Tim 3:16, NIV). It would be a great loss for the Bible to be missing a book that God wanted all Christians to profit from, and (depending on its contents), it could be quite harmful for the Bible to include a book that God did *not* inspire. However, either the Catholic Church has added seven non-inspired books—called the deuterocanonicals (Tobit, Baruch, Judith, Wisdom, Sirach, and 1 and 2 Maccabees)—or Protestantism has removed seven inspired books.[1] Fortunately, Catholics and Protestants both agree on the twenty-seven books of the New Testament. Though as we will see, several of these New Testament books were challenged by one of the Reformers and for many years were in danger of being removed from the Protestant canon as well.

A Brief History of the Canon

Entire books are dedicated to exploring the history of the canon and tracing it from the early centuries of the Church to the Protestant Reformation in the 1500s. For a Christian to understand the arguments that I will present in this chapter, however, only a brief background is needed.

Catholics and Protestants agree that after the death of the last Apostle, John, around the year 100, no more books were inspired by God. Thus the books that should be included in the Bible had all been written by around the end of the first century. At that point, it would have been nice if the list of inspired books had dropped down from Heaven on a piece of glowing, indestructible parchment. But God did not send us the canon in such a way. Instead, He did something even more miraculous; He guided the leaders of His Church into agreement. But not right away. What we see from the first 400 years of the Church's existence are many different proposed canonical lists: some missing books from what would become the New Testament, some with books that would later be rejected from it, and likewise some adding or removing books from the Old Testament.

Of the twenty-seven books in the New Testament, seven were not universally accepted as inspired in the early centuries of the Church: Hebrews, James, Jude, 2 Peter, 2 and 3 John, and (in the East) Revelation. Additionally, four books not accepted today were held by some to be inspired: the Shepherd of Hermas, the Apocalypse of Peter, the Epistle of Barnabas, and the first Epistle of Clement. In the East, the book of Revelation's inspiration was doubted as late as 380 by Cyril of Jerusalem and Gregory Nazianzen, probably as a reaction against its use by the Montanist heretics. By the mid-to-late 300s, however, a consensus had emerged within the Church that rejected the four spurious books and accepted the twenty-seven books of the New Testament we have today.

The Old Testament has a cloudier story: the Protestant canon lists thirty-nine books while the Catholic canon lists forty-three. The seven deuterocanonical books were not *universally* attested to in the first 400 years of the Church. The varying canons during these centuries sometimes included them, sometimes did not, and sometimes included only a few of the books. Like with the New Testament, it was not until the late 300s that a consensus emerged on the Old Testament canon. In the year 382, the Council of Rome (which was a regional rather than ecumenical council), convened by Pope Damasus I, drew up canonical lists for the entire Bible, which accepted all seven deuterocanonicals as inspired Scripture as well as the twenty-seven books of the New Testament. In the next decade, the regional councils in North Africa at Hippo (393) and at Carthage (397) proposed identical canons.

A regional council does not have the authority of an ecumenical council, so these synods of North Africa sent their proceedings to Pope Siricius for confirmation of the canon. We know that he confirmed it by the fact that a few years later, Pope Innocent I sent a letter to the Bishop of Toulouse containing the same seventy-three–book canon as was drawn up by the regional councils.[2]

In the early 400s, Jerome made a landmark translation of the Bible into the Latin Vulgate, and this Bible contained the seventy-three books of the Catholic canon. Jerome *personally* considered six of the deuterocanonicals as below the universally attested books of the Old Testament, though it seems he accepted Baruch as on par with them. He was one of several saints or Church Fathers who proposed canons of Scripture and offered opinions on the relative value and inspiration of specific books. The ultimate decision as to which of these canons was the accurate one had to be made by Christ's Church, led by the Holy Spirit and protected from error in her teachings on the faith.

The seventy-three–book canon drawn up by the councils and confirmed by the Pope was considered by the Church to be the true one, and Jerome humbly submitted his own personal opinion to that of the Church (as all the saints have done). From this time onward, the canon of Scripture was settled, but not *dogmatically*, for there was no need to declare the teaching dogma at the time. Fast forward 1,000 years to the 1400s, at which time the seventeenth ecumenical council convened in Florence and affirmed the Catholic canon of seventy-three inspired books. Though this decree also was not dogmatic, it was a reaffirmation—this time in an ecumenical council—of the same canon that had been used for over a millennium.

This brings us to the time of the Protestants, nearly a century later. By the end of the Reformation, three of the four main Protestant movements would be using a sixty-six–book canon, the exception being the Anglicans who kept the deuterocanonicals books in a position just shy of the rest of Scripture. Around this same time, the Catholic Church convened the ecumenical council in Trent and dogmatically defined the seventy-three–book canon.

Martin Luther's Rejection of Four New Testament Books

Martin Luther was excommunicated in the year 1521.[3] The following year, he published his New Testament but relegated four of the books to the end with this preface: "Up to this point we have had to do with the true and certain chief books of the New Testament. The four which follow have from ancient times had a different reputation."[4] Hebrews, James, Jude, and Revelation were the books whose inspiration he rejected.

It might appear at first that Luther was merely trying to be historically accurate here. However, it is clear that Luther denied the inspiration of these books for primarily theological, not historical reasons. Sure, the historical fact that these four books had not been universally attested to by the early Church made his claims more palatable. In truth, these books either contained teachings that directly contradicted the novel doctrines he was proposing (like *sola fide*), or he simply did not think much of them. If he had rejected them for historical reasons, he should have also rejected 2 Peter and 2 and 3 John, which like the other four were not universally attested to in the first centuries of the Church. To do this, however, would have been equivalent to admitting that the Church (whether by first-century dissension or sixteenth-century dogma) held at least *some* authority over canon selection. His solution was to override historical concerns altogether and appeal to no authority but his own personal discernment. Here is an excerpt from his introduction to James and Jude:

> I do not regard it as the writing of an apostle; and my reasons follow. In the first place it is flatly against Paul and all the rest of Scripture in ascribing justification to works....This fault, therefore, proves that this epistle is not the work of any apostle....But this James does nothing more than drive to the law and to its works....He mangles the Scriptures and thereby opposes Paul and all

Scripture....Therefore, I will not have him in my Bible to
be numbered among the true chief books.

Concerning the epistle of Jude, no one can deny that it is
an extract or copy of Peter's second epistle, so very like it
are all the words. He also speaks of the apostles like a
disciple who comes long after them and cites sayings and
incidents that are found nowhere else in the Scriptures.[5]

So Luther submitted the books of the Bible to his own doctrine
and found them incompatible with it.[6] Even though this particular
assertion of Luther's did not carry the day, the majority of his opinions *did* catch on with the Protestant Reformation as a whole and
formed the basis for its common doctrines.

If Protestantism is true, then there is no reason why someone today
could not remove any number of books from the New Testament
and declare that he has come up with the true Bible, made up of
whichever books do not contradict his beliefs. After all, the first
leader of the Protestant Reformation did just that to a thousand-
year-old canon, and most of the rest of his teachings and opinions
are now followed by hundreds of millions of Protestant Christians.
And certainly countless sects and cults have since then followed his
example—adding, deleting, and "retranslating" to the nth degree.
Several (excellent and valuable) Protestant cult-watch groups are
kept busy by these modern-day "reformers."

The Seven Deuterocanonical Books

At the beginning of this chapter, we left the story of the canon at
the point when the Protestant Reformation began. As we saw from
the previous section, Martin Luther was not afraid to challenge the
books comprising the New Testament. Though his alterations of
the canon of Scripture didn't ultimately spread across all of the
Protestant movements, his changes proposed to the Old Testament
did, and by the end of the Reformation, Protestantism had removed
the seven deuterocanonicals.

The Protestants rejected these books primarily because one in
particular, 2 Maccabees, included a laudatory reference to prayers
for the dead—a teaching which had been encouraged in the Catho-

lic Church for the souls in purgatory. Recall that one of the abuses that Luther had protested against was the sale of indulgences to remove the temporal punishment due for already forgiven sins—punishment that must be paid before a soul would be fit to enter Heaven. Luther and the Reformers rejected purgatory, so all that was connected with it also had to go: indulgences, prayers for the dead, and the communion of saints (which includes those both living and asleep in Christ). Second Maccabees praised the practice of praying for the souls of the dead, and it was disposed of.

Some might object that the Reformers rejected these books not for theological reasons but because they were not included in the Jewish Hebrew Bible. Thus, their historical basis was the dealbreaker, not their teachings that ran counter to Protestantism. After all, around the year 90, the Jews at Jamnia rejected these deuterocanonical books.

To answer these claims, a little more history is needed. The Septuagint was the first translation into popular Greek of the Hebrew Old Testament and was used during Jesus's time. It is the most ancient translation of the Old Testament that we have today, actually used to correct the errors that crept into the latest existing Hebrew version, which dates from the sixth century. The Septuagint was translated from more ancient and accurate Hebrew versions, which we do not have today. Further, the Septuagint was accepted as authoritative by the Jews of Alexandria and then by all Jews in Greek-speaking countries. Before Christ was incarnated, it was used extensively in the Near East by rabbis, and in the first century after Christ established His Church, the Apostles quoted prophecies from it in the books that became the New Testament. And this Septuagint *contained* the deuterocanonical books. Further, historical evidence shows that there were multiple, conflicting Jewish canons at the time of Christ; there was not one authoritative, closed canon used by Jews everywhere. Thus the argument that Christians should base their Old Testament off of the Hebrew Bible rather than the Greek Septuagint is dubious.[7]

Still, some might say, should we be reading books as canonical to the Hebrew Bible if they weren't written in Hebrew? But some of the seven deuterocanonical books, in fact, were originally written in Hebrew and only later translated into Greek and other languages.

Judith and Sirach are two such books. In the nineteenth and twentieth centuries, manuscripts written in Hebrew of Sirach were found amounting to two-thirds of the entire work, including one pre-Christian manuscript.[8] These Hebrew manuscripts had not yet been found at the time of the Protestant Reformation, and one might hope that Luther would have taken them into account. Their subsequent discovery, though, nonetheless cuts the legs out from under the objection that the seven deuterocanonical books should be excluded because they were not originally written in Hebrew. Besides Judith and Sirach, it is highly probable that other deuterocanonical books (such as Baruch, Tobit, and 1 Maccabees) were also originally written in Hebrew, though no existing Hebrew manuscripts have been found to date.

Several problems also emerge from accepting as authoritative the Jewish council's decision at Jamnia at the end of the first century. Firstly, these Jewish leaders had no authority to make a decision binding upon the Christian Church. The Jews at Jamnia had rejected Christ as God, let us not forget. Those who had accepted Christ had already become Christians. The remainder certainly had no rightful authority to decide anything about divine truth, as that authority had passed to those filled with the Holy Spirit (like the Apostles). Secondly, the Jews at Jamnia also recommended that Ezekiel, a book firmly accepted by all Christians as inspired, be "withdrawn" from the Jewish readings.[9] Yet no Christian takes their advice on that.

Finally, it should be pointed out that Protestants seeking to defend their canon based on historical evidence, even if they are convinced they have found sufficient proof, run into the problem that nowhere in the Scriptures does it say that this is the way to know which books belong in the canon. Such a criterion for choosing the canon contradicts *sola Scriptura* itself, because it is an extra-biblical principle. A consistent Protestant argument for selecting the canon of Scripture, then, must itself come from the Scriptures (which creates a circular argument). Unfortunately (but certainly providentially), no such instructions from God exist. Authority is our only appeal.

A Protestant might object on a practical level that no critical doctrines are lost by rejecting these seven books, so it does not matter much either way whether they are included or excluded from the Bible. However, the principle at stake is what is important. The seven deuterocanonical books are just one manifestation of a greater issue. Doctrine follows the canon, not the other way around, so we can't be sure what we've gained *or* lost unless we are certain about the scope of the canon.

If Protestantism is true, then for 1,500 years all of Christianity used a Bible that contained seven fully disposable, possibly deceptive books, which God did not inspire. He did, however, allow His Church to wrongly include these books as sacred Scripture, developing false teachings like purgatory from their contents, and receive comfort from those teachings. Eventually, God's chosen Reformer, Martin Luther, was able to straighten out the error concerning the Old Testament, even though his evaluation of the New Testament was greatly flawed.

Accepting the Canon from an Apostate Church

As we have previously discussed, Protestants believe that the Church "went off the rails" and into serious error some time after the first century. In other words, the visible Church became apostate, and *that* corrupted Church is what we call the Catholic Church today. The real Church was hidden for all of those centuries, invisible and waiting to be purified by the Reformation.

I have heard one Protestant pastor declare that the Church fell into significant error in the late second century. Others maintain that it was in the third or fourth century. It is understandable to see why they think so. During these early centuries, the Church Fathers penned many writings—which we still have today—that talk about the Church's teachings on the communion of saints (including asking for the intercession and prayers of the saints in Heaven), baptismal regeneration, Christ's real presence in the Eucharist, the primary authority of the church of Rome, and even purgatory and prayers for the dead.[10] None of these doctrines are taught by Protestants today, yet it is undeniable that the Church in its early centuries believed them. So if the Church went off the rails, she did so right out of the station.

Recall that the canon was not settled until the late fourth century. Until that time, there were many different canonical lists that were proposed. So we run into the intractable problem that Protestants must simultaneously believe that the Church had fallen into *serious* error by the fourth century yet also correctly identified the exact God-inspired books to be included in the New Testament. This apostate Church, which had demonstrated such egregious failings, was nonetheless to be trusted with faithfully listening to God in choosing the books that He had inspired? Such a position would be unreasonable. And indeed, as they consider the Old Testament books identified by the Church at the time, Protestants do believe that the Church erred by wrongly including seven of them. Suddenly, Martin Luther's rejection of four New Testament books doesn't seem so inappropriate. After all, if the Church had made such a blunder in the Old Testament canon, there was no reason to believe that she had gotten the New Testament right.

Some Protestants seek to get around this problem by proposing that God miraculously preserved His Church from error when choosing the New Testament canon but did not do so on other matters. God knew that we needed to know with certainty that the books of the New Testament were inspired by Him, and so He intervened in a special way in guiding even the corrupt bishops of the Catholic Church to correctly select the books.

While this claim could conceivably be true, it leads to another question: if God worked infallibly through fallible human beings—in particular through those Catholic bishops and priests who discerned the books of the original canon and then 1,100 years later through the fallible Protestant Reformers in their rejection of eleven and finally seven of those books—then why not also miraculously preserve His Church from error in her other teachings on the Faith? If God did the former, why not consider that He did the latter? It is an *ad hoc* decision (one not applicable in any larger sense) to accept that God preserved from error the Church's selection of the canon but reject the Catholic belief that He preserved her other teachings.

We can put this argument into a simple syllogism:

1. Certainty cannot rest on doubt. You cannot trust the action more than the agent.

2. The Church is the agent who defined the canon.

3. You cannot have more trust in the canon than you have in the Church.

4. Protestants do not trust the Church with even a moderate amount of certainty.

5. Therefore Protestants cannot trust the canon with even moderate certainty.[11]

If Protestantism is true, then the corrupted Church of the fourth century, which taught heresy on fundamental issues of the Faith, should nonetheless be trusted to have correctly discerned the canon of the New Testament.

The Myth of the Self-Authenticating Canon

The Reformers, of course, were not unaware of these arguments arrayed against Protestants with regard to the canon of Scripture, and they had a ready response. John Calvin was the most influential proponent of this theory, the self-authenticating canon.

By this explanation, which books are inspired and which are not is obvious to any true Christian. You don't need to accept that the Church discerned it nor have any reliance on the actual (messy) history of the canon's discernment. Rather, you as a faithful Christian can pick up your Bible, read the books, and listen for the inner witness of the Spirit telling you whether the books are inspired by God. Similarly, you could theoretically pick up another letter from the first or second century, read it, and fail to receive the Spirit's confirmation of its inspiration. Calvin described his theory of the self-authenticating canon thusly:

> But a most pernicious error widely prevails that Scripture has only so much weight as is conceded to it by the consent of the church....It is utterly vain, then, to pretend that the power of judging Scripture so lies with the church and that its certainty depends upon churchly assent. Thus, while the church receives and gives its seal of approval to the Scriptures, it does not thereby render authentic what is otherwise doubtful or controversial....As to their question—How can we be assured that this has sprung from God unless we have recourse to the decree

> of the church?—it is as if someone asked: Whence will
> we learn to distinguish light from darkness, white from
> black, sweet from bitter? Indeed, Scripture exhibits fully
> as clear evidence of its own truth as white and black
> things do of their color, or sweet and bitter things do of
> their taste....those whom the Holy Spirit has inwardly
> taught truly rest upon Scripture, and Scripture indeed is
> self-authenticated.[12]

Calvin makes two claims in these passages: firstly, that the
Church does not give authority to the Scriptures but rather the
Scriptures have authority by the fact that God inspired them; secondly, that a Christian can know the canon from the Holy Spirit's
testimony within him and not by trusting a decision of the Church.
Additionally, a Christian can know what is inspired and what is not
as easily as distinguishing "white from black, sweet from bitter."

The first claim has never been contested by the Catholic Church,
the Orthodox Churches, or any Christian community: it is a
"strawman" that Calvin seemed to think was a teaching of the
Catholic Church. But the Catholic Church's unchanging teaching is
that she *received* the Scriptures from God and was guided by Him in
discerning which books He had inspired and which He had not. The
Church is the servant of the truth and not its master.

Calvin's second claim has become the common Protestant answer to how one knows the canon of Scripture. And surely the Holy Spirit does witness to our spirits when we read the Bible. But
Calvin sets up a false dichotomy here: either the Church by discerning the canon imagines herself in authority over the Scriptures *or* the
canon is self-evident to any Christian. Calvin forces his listeners to
choose between these statements, but in fact they are both false.
Calvin replaces the belief that God guided *the Church* in selecting the
canon with the belief that God guided *me* or *you* in selecting it.
There is no principled reason to believe that God would guide me
but not guide the Church in this discernment.

Additionally, Calvin's subjective criterion for book canonization
is surely impractical and unrealistic. How would a person seeking
truth but not yet indwelt by the Holy Spirit know which books to
read to find truth? What about a new Christian who has not yet
learned to discern a wise inner voice from those of his own anxie-

ties? At what point would a Christian be considered ready to help define the canon, and if two disagreed, whose inner judgment would be considered correct?

Another problem with Calvin's claim is that the facts of history flatly contradict it. As we have seen, the selection of the canon was not an easy, clear process without debate that ended in the early second century. Rather, the canon slowly emerged through a laborious process, with differing canons being proposed by different Church Fathers during these centuries. These faithful, Spirit-filled men proposed *different* canons. If the canon were obvious and self-evident, the Holy Spirit would have individually led each of these faithful disciples to the same canon. It was not until almost 400 that the canon was settled, and it contained the seventy-three books of the Catholic Bible. Over 1,100 years later, the Reformers changed the canon by rejecting the seven deuterocanonical books, another example of intelligent and faithful men disagreeing about the "obvious" canon.

If Protestantism is true, then the canon is obvious to any true Christian bright enough to discern black from white. Therefore many (supposedly) holy men and women who gave their lives for Christ in the early centuries of the Church did not actually have the Holy Spirit, for they were not able to apprehend the true canon of Scripture. If the canon is known easily by the Spirit testifying to the Christian's heart, it must be concluded that not until Martin Luther, John Calvin, and the other Protestant Reformers in the sixteenth century did true Christian leaders exist who listened to the Holy Spirit on this topic.

The "Fallible Collection" and Reasonable Certainty

The historical realities of the canon of Scripture leave Protestants in a pickle as to how they can know with certainty that the sixty-six books in their Bibles are *the* correct set of inspired books. They need to know with the strongest certainty possible, because they hold to *sola Scriptura*—that from the Bible alone comes all of the saving truths that God revealed for man to believe and live by. But if they are not certain that the books contained in their Bible are all inspired by God nor that they haven't left some inspired books out, then suddenly all of the saving truths that they have gleaned from these books are up again for debate. Worse yet, they could be missing some important saving truths!

This unsettling reality is why many Protestants are not comfortable with Protestant pastor R.C. Sproul's well-known description of the Bible as a "fallible collection of infallible books."[13] If the canon of Scripture is not inerrant, then there is no use claiming that each of the books themselves is inerrant. Sproul rightly recognized that he had no principled reason to believe that the all-too fallible Church of the early centuries correctly selected the books of the Bible or that the very fallible Protestant Reformers of the sixteenth century were correct in their canon, either. Hence his supremely unsatisfactory formula has become an uncomfortable perch upon which some Protestants try to find rest from answering the question of the canon.

Knowing the canon with "reasonable" certainty is still good enough for many Protestants. After all, they argue, the Church got the New Testament canon (which is the most important one) completely right. And we can all feel some sympathy with this perspective.

The main problem with this position is that it accepts the opinions of the Church Fathers and the decision of the Church herself on the canon while simultaneously considering them to have gravely erred on other fundamental issues of the Faith. (See the discussion on accepting the canon from the apostate Church, earlier, for more about this.) It is an inescapable and unanswerable problem for Protestantism, striking at its very root.

If Protestantism is true, then the basis for all of our Christian beliefs, the Bible, very likely contains books which God did not inspire or leaves out books which He did inspire. At best we can be *somewhat* sure that *many* of the books of the Bible are *probably* inspired, but we do not have even reasonable certainty that all of the books of the Bible are inspired nor that it is not missing inspired books. According to the influential Protestant voice of Sproul, the canon was not infallibly selected. Thus it may very well be erroneous. It may contain error. That's an unsettling thought. Because if Protestantism is true, the Bible is all we've got.

Sola Scriptura's Logical Consequences

As we have discussed, Protestants hold that Christians should base their beliefs off of the Bible alone. Traditions can be accepted which do not contradict the Scriptures, but only in the Bible are found the saving truths that God wished to communicate to His children. All of Christianity, therefore, should use the (Protestant) Bible as their source for faith. Only in the Bible are found the inerrant words of God, completely trustworthy and true. While some good teachings can be found outside of it, none are on anywhere near the same level as the God-breathed Scriptures. Therefore, they conclude, the Church should *always* have based its teachings off of the Bible alone.

This (extra-biblical) belief has several problems. Firstly, as we have seen, in the early centuries of the Church, many different canonical lists were used, some containing books which were ultimately determined to be noncanonical. So the Church was using at least some books that God had not inspired during her first four centuries and in fact was not even certain about which books were inspired until the late fourth century. Secondly, the canon selected at that time was the seventy-three–book Catholic set, and it was many centuries later that the Protestant Reformers "corrected" the erroneous list by removing the deuterocanonical books, which means that Christ's Church for most of her history had been using the *wrong* set of books, including seven that God did not inspire. Yet all this time, according to *sola Scriptura*, the Church and all Christians were supposed to have been basing their beliefs on the Bible alone.

Additionally, we would expect the different movements within Protestantism to all agree in their interpretations of Scripture, since they were all using the correct canon for the first time in Christian history *and* were finally basing their beliefs off of the Bible alone, without man-made traditions tainting their teachings. Yet the historical reality is completely the opposite. Countless disagreements on doctrine rapidly built up in every place where Protestantism took hold: Luther's own compatriots disagreed with many of his teachings; Zwingli's colleagues disagreed with him; the radical Reformers (Anabaptists) contradicted all of the magisterial Reformers; Calvin contradicted Luther, Zwingli, and the radicals; and the Anglicans incorporated a hodge-podge of the continental Reformers' ideas into their own unique blend of Catholic-Protestant teachings.

Though all of these Protestant groups' adherents had received the Holy Spirit and were honestly doing their best to follow what they thought God was saying in the Scriptures, they came to different interpretations on almost every important issue of the faith. The Anabaptists in particular highlight the fundamental problem with *sola Scriptura*: at both Wittenberg in Germany where Luther was active and Zurich where Zwingli lived, the radical Reformers arose, accusing both Luther and Zwingli of compromising the "pure biblical truths" with human traditions by valuing the works of the early Church Fathers (like Augustine and Origen) as well as Church councils like Nicaea in interpreting Scripture.

The Anabaptists rightly noticed that there was no explicit mention in the New Testament of baptizing infants, a practice which had been done in the Church since the beginning and which Luther and Zwingli accepted as orthodox, arguing that while not mentioned outright in the Bible, it certainly was harmonious with the Bible. The fact that this practice was part of traditional Christian orthodoxy (or sacred Tradition) was not good enough for the Anabaptists, who rejected infant baptism and rebaptized all Christians who joined their group (Anabaptist means rebaptizer).

But the Anabaptists did not stop there: based on their readings of the Scriptures, Christians should isolate themselves from the world. Private property was rejected on the grounds that the Bible said that the early Christians held everything in common. Many radical Reformers also began to rethink the dogma of the Trinity: they argued that the traditional understanding of the Trinity was not explicitly stated in the Bible and was a later invention of theologians. One historian records, "Anti-trinitarianism, already evident in the late 1520s, became a hallmark of the [Anabaptist] movement in the 1550s, causing widespread concern in both Protestant and Catholic circles."[14] For the Anabaptists, *sola Scriptura* meant relying on *no* tradition from the early centuries of Christianity (other than the tradition of the canon of Scripture, an inconsistency they apparently didn't consider). The magisterial Reformers, however, thought that the Anabaptists had gone too far: the Church Fathers and Councils could "generally" be relied upon to come to a faithful interpretation of the Scriptures. But who could say which of these sets of Protestant groups was correct? Which of these differing ideas of what *sola Scriptura* meant was the true definition?

No honest religious historian can deny that the result of *sola Scriptura* has been doctrinal chaos. And over the past 500 years, Protestant churches have continually fragmented from one another over differing interpretations of the Bible. The number of distinct Protestant communities (or "denominations") is in the thousands and continues to grow.

If Protestantism is true, then Christians should base their beliefs off of the Bible alone and, with the guidance of the Holy Spirit, be able to come to know the fullness of the truth revealed by Christ. But how, then, are we to explain the thousands of Protestant denominations, each with its own biblical interpretation?

The Canon of Shakespeare

To shore up my foggy high-school memories from English class, I bought a copy of the complete works of William Shakespeare. While reading the introduction, I was surprised to learn that compiling such a volume was not a straightforward task because the "canon" of Shakespeare's works has been (and still is) a contested issue: literary scholars differ in which works are fully his, which contain others' contributions, and which are not his at all but only attributed to him.

This fact surprised me, because Shakespeare died less than 400 years ago and was very popular and well-known even while he was still alive. Yet the canon of Scripture presents much greater difficulties: its books were written over the course of many centuries, with the last book, Revelation, having been written almost two *millennia* ago. We do not have the first-century originals of the New Testament manuscripts nor complete second-century copies of them. We do not even have complete third-century copies. In fact, only from the fourth century do we have two nearly complete biblical manuscripts: the *Codex Vaticanus* and the *Codex Sinaiticus*.

The Old Testament of the *Codex Sinaiticus* is in the Greek Septuagint version and contains some of the seven deuterocanonical books as well as a few books included in its New Testament that the Church determined later in the fourth century to lack inspiration (the Epistle of Barnabas and The Shepherd of Hermas). The *Codex Vaticanus* also includes the deuterocanonical books, but several books from the New Testament are missing, probably due to the manuscript's deterioration over the centuries or possibly because they were just never included in this version. It also seems possible that it contained noncanonical writings like first Clement. Here again we have evidence of the canon of Scripture still being determined as late as the mid-300s.

If we have trouble figuring out which books Shakespeare did and did not author just a few hundred years ago, how are we to have any certainty as to which books God inspired in the Old and New Testaments thousands of years ago? Even these two oldest of discovered biblical manuscripts were copies of copies of the originals written long after the Apostles had all died. We know that the Church's bishops debated, discussed, argued, and prayed to discern which books should be in the canon, so it was through *human effort* that God led us to know the inspired books. Given that human effort was involved in the selection of the canon in a messy process spanning hundreds of years, it is impossible to escape the fact that, as Christians living so many centuries later, we must use reason as well as place our faith in God's goodness for conscience-binding assurance of having the true canon.

As a Protestant, I was naturally inclined to believe the Protestant arguments for why the sixty-six-book canon in my Bible was the right one. The arguments I read for why the Reformers excluded the deuterocanonical books seemed believable enough to me then, and I understand why they seem plausible to Protestants. But let's be honest, even humanly speaking, those arguments are no more convincing than the reasons for why Catholics *included* those books. Like with puzzling out the canon of Shakespeare's works, the reasoned arguments for accepting or rejecting the disputed books of the Bible can only take one so far. Ultimately, to believe that we have *all* the books and *exactly* the books in our Bible that God worked so miraculously to inspire, we have to believe that God led *someone* or *some* group of people to accurately discern the truth. Historical reasoning alone is simply insufficient.

Consider this passage from the letter of Jude—a book accepted as inspired by all Christians: "But when the archangel Michael, contending with the devil, disputed about the body of Moses..." (Jude 9). Nowhere in the Old Testament do we encounter this story. Instead, it comes from a Jewish legend called *The Assumption of Moses*. Adding even more obscurity to this reference is the fact that the extant version of this legend cuts off *before* Moses's death, so the sole way we know that this reference is from that work is because the Church Fathers, who presumably had the entire text available to them at the time, tell us so.[15]

But that is not the end of the peculiarities in this letter from Jude. A short while later, Jude quotes from the Jewish apocryphal work 1 Enoch! Add to these legendary and apocryphal references the fact that we don't know which Jude, exactly, wrote this letter. We can rule out Judas Iscariot of course, and it doesn't seem likely it was Jude the Apostle. There were other Judes in the early Church, and the one most scholars think wrote it was the Jude mentioned in Matthew 13:55 as a kinsman of Jesus. So Jude's brother, then, was likely the James who became a patriarch of Jerusalem in the early Church.

Given these dubious elements of the letter, it is not surprising that the canonical status of Jude was disputed for centuries in the early Church. Its canonicity was not definitively confirmed until the fourth and fifth centuries. In Syriac Christianity, doubts remained about the letter until the Middle Ages. And recall that Martin Luther himself dismissed Jude as uninspired from the first edition of his Bible translation. Luther knew that it was strongly disputed in the early Church and claimed that reason in his attempt to remove it from the canon.

The inclusion of Jude in the Bible is just one example of the complex decisions made by the Church in discerning the canon of Scripture. For me, this realization that we just can't know everything historically and must trust God's guidance led to asking this question: do I believe that God guided the early Church in selecting the canon, or do I believe that He let the early Church choose erroneous books but then guided Martin Luther and the other Reformers (who lived just before Shakespeare in the sixteenth century) to correct those errors and finally give Christianity the true canon? I came to the conclusion that God guided His Church's discernment of those books over the centuries so that all people throughout all ages would have the deposit of faith preserved uncorrupted, that we might then know Christ in truth and find salvation in Him.

If Protestantism is true, then God miraculously preserved His Word, yes, but only after letting all of His children believe in a faulty Bible for 1,500 years. Not until shortly before Shakespeare's time, the beginning of the modern era in history, did God finally guide a group of Christians to accurately select the books of the canon. He was *very* slow in keeping His promise to lead the Church into all truth (see John 16:13), a truth not fully intended for all Christians but specifically for the subset of those living after the sixteenth century.

Chapter Six
The Reformers' Legacy: Protestantism Today

It's been almost 500 years since the Reformation was launched. What is the legacy of the Protestant Reformers today? Well, as can be expected of any group of people sincerely trying to follow Christ, there is a lot of good news to report! The Protestants have produced beautiful spiritual artwork, life-changing Bible studies and curricula, enduring political action for the good of all people, and courageous acts of faith that make me proud to call them my family. Many (if not most) Protestants are devoted to their Savior, whom they love. It's not the validity of Protestants, of course, that I am arguing against here. It's the validity of the claims that were made in their name half a century ago—claims of which many may be unaware.

But certainly we can tell something of the meat of these claims by their fruit. When we look at the sociology that has developed out of Protestantism over time, what do we find? We now have millions of Christians who call themselves Lutherans, Calvinists, or Anglicans, as well as Baptists, Methodists, Pentecostals, and "nondenominational" Christians—just to name a few of the myriad Protestant communities. Yet, depending on which Protestant community you talk to, it's either never been better or never been worse. Old denominational loyalties are weakening and dissolving, many Christians are seeking churches in the same way that they shop for electronic gadgets, and enormous megachurches attract thousands every week to their stadium-like arenas.

Once someone has found his way into one of these Christian communities, his search for the truth has not ended but really only just begun. As I discovered when converting from atheism to Evangelical Protestantism, there were more differences among Christian groups than I ever would have imagined. And each group—claiming various levels of authority—believed they were teaching the truth as revealed by God. The options within Protestantism were overwhelming. Depending upon what you believe on any given issue of the faith, some Protestant community will probably align with you (and many others will oppose you). Many denominations have their own seminaries, colleges, and publishing houses, all based on their particular beliefs and priorities.

The Protestant spectrum now covers a wide swath of contradictory beliefs: infant versus believer baptism, Christ present in some way in the Eucharist or symbolically only, the indissolubility of marriage or the acceptability of divorce, the condemning of abortion as murder or the accepting of abortion as permissible, the ordination of women or of men only, the Trinity as one God in three Persons or as one God Person with three purposes. There are differences on predestination and free will, whether salvation can be lost, whether same-sex "marriage" is valid, and so on. Take "speaking in tongues" for example. Depending on your denomination, it *could* be a sign that you're gifted, deluded, possessed, or even finally saved.

So unfortunately, even amid much spiritual wealth, there is doctrinal chaos in Protestantism. From the beginning, there was no way to resolve disputing biblical interpretations among Protestant factions, and that problem has magnified through the centuries, resulting in what we see today. Since there is no authority that can definitively decide how the Scriptures are to be interpreted, Protestants are left to shoulder the burden of not only interpreting for themselves but also of determining which particular group of persons share their interpretation. And that is then their denomination.

Even the most sacred truths, never imagined to be challenged by the Reformers, are not only being questioned but denied outright, further fracturing the already divided Protestants. One of the foremost among these truths being attacked today is the tradition of marriage between one man and one woman, which brings us to the first topic of this chapter.

The Protestant Meltdown over Questions of Sexuality

Same-sex relationships, long considered by the Church to be sinful aberrations, are now becoming accepted by many as normal. Persons with same-sex attraction have become a vocal minority and have successfully pushed for legislation recognizing their relationships as civil unions and even "marriage," at the same time overturning many laws which supported traditional marriage. They have fought for acceptance of their same-sex relationships within society and have been winning it at every level, using the media, the academy, the courts, and the legislatures to promote their agenda.

No Christian church ever recognized the morality of homosexual relationships or the validity of same-sex "marriages" until late in the twentieth century. But now, within all large Protestant communities, same-sex factions have emerged and begun fighting for reversals of their community's long-held teachings on the sanctity of marriage as being between one man and one woman. With the growing acceptance of homosexuality in society, these groups have gained power and influence and are now whelming entire Protestant denominations. In this section, we will focus especially on the Lutherans and Anglicans, two groups that trace their lineage directly to the Reformation itself.

The Evangelical Lutheran Church in America (ELCA) is the largest set of Lutheran communities in the United States with over four million members. In 2009, the ELCA voted to endorse clergy who are in homosexual relationships. Lutheran Pastor Russell Saltzman strongly opposed the move and admitted that his loyalties had been challenged by it:

> The original intent of the sixteenth century Reformers wasn't to start a new church but to be a witness for evangelical reform within the one church. Our Lutheran confessional documents...forcefully argues that nothing Lutherans taught was contrary to the faith of the church catholic, nor even contrary to that faith held by the Church of Rome. As it has happened, much to our Lutheran chagrin, late twentieth century Rome itself has become a better witness to an evangelical gospel than early twenty-first century Lutherans have proved capable of being. And for all the radical Lutheran polemic coming after Augsburg—you know, about the pope being the latest anti-Christ sitting on the throne of the whore of Babylon—truth is, these days, I get far less trouble from the bishop of Rome than I get from my own bishop.[1]

The ELCA, however, is simply following in the footsteps of the Episcopal Church, which is the American branch of the Anglican Communion. Rowan Williams, the Anglican Archbishop of Canterbury, requested that the leaders of the Episcopal Church not break the Communion by blessing same-sex unions in Episcopal churches or by ordaining practicing homosexuals to be bishops. The Episcopal Church responded by ignoring him and doing both. In 2003, Gene Robinson was elected bishop in spite of his ongoing homosexual relationship, and in 2009, the Episcopal Church went a step further. Anglican Bishop of Durham, N.T. (Tom) Wright (retired August 2010) vividly describes the situation: "In the slow-moving train crash of international Anglicanism, a decision taken in California has finally brought a large coach off the rails altogether. The House of Bishops of the Episcopal Church (TEC) in the United States has voted decisively to allow in principle the appointment, to all orders of ministry, of persons in active same-sex relationships. This marks a clear break with the rest of the Anglican Communion."[2]

Protestantism in its earliest days desired to reject what it thought were mere traditions of men, and endorsers of same-sex unions claim that the biblical passages denouncing homosexual acts were just that—man-made traditions that happened to be the cultural norms of the time. Isn't it possible, they claim, that the historical condemnation of homosexuality is just one more of those human traditions that our modern civilization has finally realized was wrong?

A traditional Protestant might object that the churches supporting homosexual behavior are obviously contradicting the clear meaning of the Bible. And so we are reminded of the question that won't go away: Who exactly has the authority to correctly interpret the Bible? In practice, each Protestant reads the Bible for herself, through the interpretive lens made up of her particular Protestant community's teachings, her own experiences, and whatever other books and commentaries she trusts. (The Catholic Church, on the other hand, admits that an authoritative interpreter of the Scriptures is needed and claims that the Church's Magisterium is the principal interpreter that God has established.)

Of course, many Protestant communities have not yet fractured over this issue. Notably, most of the Evangelicals. Those communities are to be commended for standing up against something false. However, the root of the problem is endemic to Protestantism itself and cannot be resolved by Evangelical resistance.

If (mainline) Protestantism is true, then the moral standards of something as fundamental, sacred, and intimate as sexual union may have been terribly misinterpreted for nearly two millennia. The Reformers would never have imagined that their churches would one day be blessing homosexual unions and calling them marriages, which shows how far the Reformers' descendants have drifted from their spiritual roots.

The Protestant Flip-Flop on Other Moral Issues

The question of practicing homosexual clergy and same-sex "marriage" are just the latest moral issues to confront Protestantism. In the early twentieth century, all Protestant communities taught that contraception was immoral, but beginning with the Anglican Church at their 1930 Lambeth Conference, one by one they've changed their teachings and declared contraception an acceptable, moral course of action. At first, it was only considered good to use in special circumstances, but soon it became permissible and even laudable in most any situation. Few Protestants today even think to question whether contraception is sinful. Their parents used it, and everyone else they know uses it. The Bible doesn't say that it is immoral, so it must be up to each Christian's conscience to decide. The Catholic Church stands today virtually alone in condemnation of contraception and sterilization as immoral.

Similarly, up until the 1960s, all Protestant communities condemned abortion as evil, but as the winds of modern society began to shift, so did these communities' teachings. Large groups of Presbyterians, Methodists, Episcopalians, Lutherans, and even Southern Baptists reversed their teachings and declared that abortion was permissible in some or all cases.[3] (It should be noted, however, that the Southern Baptist Convention in later years reversed its decision and reaffirmed its condemnation of abortion, to its credit.) Abortion, the direct killing of an unborn human person, is now condoned by many Protestant communities, representing millions of Christians. The Catholic Church continues its unchanging witness to the sanctity of human life from conception to natural death by condemning abortion unequivocally.

Marriage was once considered an indissoluble bond by all Christians, but like with contraception, sterilization, and abortion, most Protestant communities have now reversed their teachings on the impossibility of divorce and remarriage, allowing their members to remarry so long as they have gotten a civil divorce from their former spouse.

When the Protestant Reformers threw out most of the seven sacraments, the theology behind marriage was fundamentally damaged, leading to the current state of divorce and remarriage within Protestant churches. The Catholic Church recognizes that a true marriage is indissoluble, so a couple who were married (even in another Christian church) are considered to be truly married unless and until an investigation into the circumstances by which the marriage was entered into by the couple is conducted and finds that there were obstacles that prevented a true marriage from being joined. This investigation is the annulment process. An annulled "marriage" is one that never actually occurred in God's eyes—the two people never became one flesh—and thus both persons are free to become married to someone else. The circumstances that could impede a marriage from occurring are beyond the scope of this book, but suffice it to say that the Catholic Church takes the biblical words of Jesus Christ seriously; a marriage is not annulled due merely to "irreconcilable differences" or even infidelity by one or both persons.

Our world, so deeply in need of a Christian witness to the sanctity of marriage and to the possibility of life-long marriage, instead sees the rampant divorce and remarriage among Christians as proof that these evils are acceptable and that God doesn't seem to help Christians stay married any more than other people. The weakening of marriage has led to the disintegration of the family, which is the fundamental cell of society. Along with contraception, which removed the necessity of children from marriage, it has paved the way for the rise of acceptance of same-sex unions and "marriages." It is no coincidence that the Catholic Church has stood like a rock, unmoved and unchanged in her moral teachings against the battering waves of the modern world with its selfish and morally relative agenda. The bishops, priests, and laity of the Catholic Church have not accomplished this feat by their own strength. Rather, the Spirit of God has disallowed the Church to teach error in faith and morals.

If Protestantism is true, then such deeply tragic and long-condemned actions as artificial contraception, abortion, and divorce are not issues settled in the mind of God but are open to reinterpretation according to the changing culture around us.

The Disintegration of Mainline Protestantism

On a weekday trip to the grocery store, I saw two bumper stickers for churches: the Powerhouse Church and the Cactus Cowboy Church. I have a friend who goes to a very hip, artsy Protestant church called Mosaic, which denies that it is a "church" in the standard sense. None of these churches fall under the usual categories, nor are they affiliated with a standard denomination. The mainline Protestant denominations are shrinking rapidly, and the coming collapse of Evangelicalism has been talked of as well,[4] so it is not surprising to see the rise of such "niche" churches. We are all looking for community, and these churches are offering community in varying ways that appeal to specific groups of people.

Ask a young adult who goes to a denominational church how he would describe himself and you will likely hear, "I am a Christian; I go to this church because they teach soundly from the Bible." He would not label himself a "Baptist" or a "Methodist." The fact that a person's parents were a certain denomination doesn't bind her nearly as strongly as it once did, when families formed communities that were often homogeneous religiously. Alister McGrath talks about this fading denominational loyalty within Protestantism: "Even as late as 1960, most Americans had serious misgivings about worshiping at Protestant denominations other than their own, feeling this compromised their religious identities. Their loyalty was primarily—and in many cases exclusively—to the specific beliefs, structure, and life of a particular denomination."[5]

If what really matters is believing in Jesus and following Him, not where you go to church or how you label yourself religiously, then people will go to the church where they can both "be fed" and contribute their God-given gifts. A cowboy is going to love it at the Cowboy church where barbecues are fired up after every Sunday service and the elder rides a horse.

Not to be flippant, but just like I have my unique Starbucks coffee—a mint mocha latte, decaf, whip—I can now have my unique church, and the people there are like me, so that's where I am going. If I don't fit into the categories of Anglican or churches of Christ or Pentecostal, I can go instead to where I have found a community who relates to my personal journey with Jesus.

Because we are now used to having our preference in just about everything, and because our Western culture is driven so strongly by consumerism, it is easy to see how these same ideas get translated into a demand for church choice. Why should I go to a church that doesn't "feed me" or that "I don't get anything out of?" I don't willingly subject myself to inconvenience and pain in other areas of my life, so why do it on Sundays? I want a church that fits my tastes, plays worship music I like, has people of the same age and demographic as me, and provides activities that I find meaningful. McGrath confirms this trend:

> With the emergence of a consumerist mentality in American Protestant culture since about 1980, the driving issue is where to find the best preaching, the best Christian education, or even the best parking facilities....The issue is not denominational identity but local pastoral excellence. In marked contrast, their grandparents would have sought out the local church of their own denomination wherever they went.[6]

At the heart of this ecclesial consumerism is a Protestant assumption that there is no visible and true Church that we all need to reunite with; rather, all churches are part of the invisible Church, each offering something unique to the menu. So choosing one over the other is like choosing a different dish at a restaurant.

The Catholic understanding is the opposite. There is a visible Church that Christ established, but Protestant communities have broken off in schism from her. Choosing a church is nothing like choosing a kitchen appliance or an espresso, nor should the focus even be on what works for "me." One should search for the Church that Christ built and to which He appointed rightful authorities (the Apostles and their successors), the Church that He promised to protect from error and lead into all truth, the Church that the gates of hell cannot prevail against, the Church that Peter led and that has made authoritative decisions on truth and heresy for millennia. Certainly *within* that Church will be people grouped by different interests and callings—there is legitimate diversity within the unity of the truth. But on Sundays, we still all kneel united before the cross of Christ and recite the one creed. Christ called us to unity, so He must desire it *and* make it possible for all types of people to unite with the Church He built.

If Protestantism is true, then no one Church has the fullness of the truth, but all churches teach a mixture of true and false doctrine. So it makes sense to find one that agrees on enough of the truth that you deem essential and also that appeals to your tastes and preferences. In addition, as your tastes change and your church feels less relevant, it's your right to find a different church that meets your needs.

"I Have No Authority But Jesus"

I listened to a set of talks given by an Evangelical Protestant pastor, whom I will call Pastor Neil, which focused on equipping men to be faithful and strong disciples of Christ. One important point he makes is the idea of *jurisdiction*. Jurisdiction, in Pastor Neil's parlance, is equivalent to authority. He rightly points out that we men, as head of our families, have authority given to us by God the Father and that we must accept this authority and use it to help lead our families in a Christ-like way. I couldn't agree more.

Notice how we all have human authorities in our lives? At home when we were children, our parents were our authorities; at school, our teachers and principals were. In civil society, we have authorities at many levels: city council, mayor, county leaders, and state and federal legislators. Do they really have authority over us, though? Yes. We see this authority when we break a law, because the police come and give us a ticket or arrest us, a judge then tries us for the crime, and we may go to jail for decades or even be executed! At work—in business or academia—we have authorities over us; I personally have six levels of supervisors above me in the authority chain going right up to the top of my company.

But what about in the Christian faith? Ah, here it is different, is it not? Here, surely, we have "no authority over us except Jesus Christ." That is exactly what hundreds of millions of Protestant Christians say when it comes to their beliefs and their church. Is that the way Christ intended us to live as Christians?

Let's now get back to what Pastor Neil has to say about authority (jurisdiction): "Pride will destroy a jurisdiction. Don't trust Mohammed nor Buddha: who gave them jurisdiction? Why should I listen to him? He doesn't have jurisdiction. Where men do not submit to their elders, there will be destruction and disorder in the church. If a man won't listen to the elders, to the church, if he won't submit to their jurisdiction, Paul says, 'I will deliver such a one to Satan' and his jurisdiction [1 Cor. 5:4–5]." He also mentions that Peter told Christians to submit to the government, superiors in the work sphere, human institutions, and authorities for the Lord's sake.

What if we were to apply his statements to Protestantism? Martin Luther and the other leaders of the Reformation did not submit to their elders, the bishops of Christ's Church, and that did indeed lead to "destruction and disorder" in the Church. It led to schism upon schism and a thousand splinterings afterward, explicitly against Christ's command and Paul's that there be no divisions among Christians.

Pastor Neil seems to mean "church" in the smallest sense possible: the group of people who meet at someone's home or who rent space at the local school on Sundays or who have built a church building. The "elders" of the church are presumably whoever founded it and became pastor plus whomever he chose as assistant pastor.

"If a man won't listen to the elders, to the church, if he won't submit to their jurisdiction, Paul says, 'I will deliver such a one to Satan' and his jurisdiction." When and how many times has this happened in Christ's Church through history? How about the Manichees? The Monophysites? The Docetists? The Arians? The Nestorians? The men who chose to reject the elders of Christ's Church and their authority were delivered to Satan and his authority. When exactly did it become okay for a Christian to throw off the yoke of authority of Christ's Church and follow his own ideas of what is true? Did Paul's words cease to apply once we reached the 1500s?

Without the one, apostolic, and universal Church that Christ established and which teaches truth in faith and morals, following the jurisdiction of someone within a church makes little sense. In practice, what often happens is that a person who disagrees with the elders just leaves and goes to the church down the street—or founds his own church in which *he is the elder!* "Now it says in the Bible that people have to listen to *me*. Otherwise they are handed over to Satan! Now *I* am the elder." We see how ridiculous these verses on unity become if Christ has no Church but only a thousand individual, divided, and often contradictory churches with a thousand different elders, all claiming some measure of rightful authority.

If Protestantism is true, then if a Christian needs spiritual authority in her life—whether to stave off the devil, fight sin, or make a moral ruling—she has myriad and confusing options. Any "elder" of any church where she feels "at home" might do. But how would she know that this elder and this church were teaching the truth of God?

Chapter Seven
Protestant Objections to the Catholic Church

Most Protestants do not have well-researched theological objections to the Catholic Church. This is no criticism; most people don't have the time or interest to research a belief system other than their own. However, while ignorance is excusable, slander is just plain unfair. I discuss here several misconceptions widely held by Protestants, ones that might come up in casual conversations with friends, or at a family reunion. These objections are often vague generalizations—which makes them even easier to believe, especially for Protestants who have grown up in an anti-Catholic milieu. Their widespread acceptance in Protestantism necessitates a response, with the hope that Catholics will be better equipped to answer such objections and that Protestants will be able to move beyond them to more substantial issues.

"The Catholic Church Manipulated Historical Texts"

One accusation Protestants often make against the Catholic Church is that throughout the centuries, her leaders systematically and maliciously altered or destroyed writings that disagreed with them in order to manipulate history and skew it favorably toward the Church. Rarely is any specific evidence provided of the times that this malfeasance has occurred, but the accusation itself suffices to lay a blanket of suspicion on any historical document or writing that contradicts Protestant beliefs, allowing a Protestant presented with such historical works to reject them outright as possible forgeries. Now certainly *some* heretical writings were destroyed at one time or another, but that was done for the protection of the faithful.

This accusation is refuted in many ways. For example, we possess the historical writings from many groups deemed heretics. We also have the writings of scores of non-Christians who wrote about the Church, how the early Christians worshipped and lived, and how society viewed them. A question for a Protestant to ask himself is, when exactly did the members of the Church begin this all-encompassing campaign to destroy and alter writings? And what actual evidence is there for this claim?

Another problem with this idea is that, if true, how does a Protestant know that *the Bible itself* was not maliciously and deceptively altered by the members of Christ's Church to change what Jesus and the Apostles really said, since according to this accusation, the Church must have had control over what writings survived and which were destroyed?

Some Protestants answer that we know the Bible has not been changed by the Catholic Church because we can use methods of textual criticism to see that there is relatively little variation among the biblical manuscripts and fragments we possess. The problem with this response is that, as was discussed in chapter five, the earliest surviving mostly complete biblical manuscripts date from the 300s. That leaves over two hundred years for the members of the Church, who hand-copied the Bible from the originals, to alter God's words to fit their own man-made traditions. If the manipulation was as systematic as some Protestants claim, the Church could have accomplished such a deception by modifying the very first copies of biblical books.

An interesting case study to the question of forged versus genuine historical writings is the work of Ignatius, bishop of Antioch, who lived from the year 50 to the early 100s, when he suffered martyrdom at the hands of the Romans. He was therefore a contemporary of the Apostles themselves. Along with Polycarp, he studied under John the Beloved Apostle himself. Seven of his letters have been confirmed as authentic, and five other letters attributed to him are known to be forgeries. The seven genuine letters contain strong evidence supporting the Catholic Church's teachings on the visibility and hierarchy of the Church. They also emphasize Christ's real presence in the Eucharist, the primacy of the Church of Rome, and the goodness of consecrated virginity for the Kingdom.[1]

Obviously the acceptance of these seven letters as authentic would be incredibly damaging to many Protestant ecclesiologies. For example, John Calvin's interpretation of the New Testament on how the Church should be governed directly contradicted Ignatius's statements about the organization and leadership of the Church: "Calvin insisted that a highly specific form of ministry was stipulated by scripture...pastors, teachers, elders, and deacons" where the elders (or "presbyters") were crucial to the church's governance.[2] Naturally, the Ignatian letters have no place in Calvin's interpretation.

In the sixteenth century, Calvin rejected *all* of the letters as fraudulent, both the five spurious ones and the seven genuine ones, and he did so in acerbic tones:

> With regard to what they pretend as to Ignatius, if they
> would have it to be of the least importance, let them
> prove that the apostles enacted laws concerning Lent,
> and other corruptions. Nothing can be more nauseating,
> than the absurdities which have been published under
> the name of Ignatius; and therefore, the conduct of those
> who provide themselves with such masks for deception
> is the less entitled to toleration.[3]

Sound and faithful scholarship from both Catholic and Protestant historians has proven Calvin to be in error here about Ignatius's letters, which means that his form of church government (the presbyteral model) must be called into question. If he erred in this important area, in what other interpretations of Scripture did he blunder?

If Protestantism is true, then many writings of the early Christians and Church Fathers directly contradict the doctrines of Protestant communities. Since their writings have been demonstrated to be authentic, either the early Christians twisted the truth given to them by the Apostles or the Protestant Reformers misinterpreted the Scriptures on many fundamental issues, erroneously teaching as truth doctrines which neither Christ nor the Apostles ever taught.

"No One is Infallible, so the Church Cannot be"

The Catholic Church makes the outlandish claim that all her teachings on faith and morals are true—that not one of them is in error. As a Protestant, when I learned about this claim, I smelled blood in the water. I knew that there was no possible way that it was true, and all I had to do was find one example of a false teaching, and the whole house of Catholic cards would come tumbling down.

Why was I so sure that the Catholic Church's claim was false? Simple: I know from human experience that every person and human institution is corrupted in some way.

For example, all people commit sins and do evil, just as the Bible says, "all have sinned and fallen short of the glory of God" because "there is none righteous, no not one" (Rom. 3:23). Additionally, every organization and institution, including the Catholic Church, is full of people who sin, and these sins must also "corrupt" the organizations. Look also at the United States government. How many scandals have there been in the past decade (or even in the past year)? Courts of law issue wrong rulings that imprison or even execute innocent persons while the guilty walk free. The Declaration of Independence says that "all men are created equal," with the right to life, and yet we enslaved African persons and now abort babies in their mothers' wombs.

Christian churches don't seem much better. How many pastors have been found doing evil things: bribery, infidelity, or worse? What about the perverted priests who abused children? As a Protestant, though I thought what my pastor taught was mostly true, I didn't necessarily agree with everything he said. Why should I? He was just another sinful, fallible human being like me.

Further, as a Protestant I believed that the Bible taught that we are *not* righteous; in fact, Christ's righteousness was only *imputed* to us by the Father such that we appear holy because He only sees His perfect Son when he looks at us. But we are still sinful and corrupted people. We are not truly made holy. (This is not the Catholic belief.)

Given the universal corruption in people and in institutions, what hubris for the Catholic Church to claim that she teaches no error! Protestant churches are at least truthful in that, though they contradict each other in many ways, none of them claim that everything they teach is true. At best they claim that the Bible is true and that they try to teach from the Bible. As I continued growing in my Protestant faith and sought to refute this wild Catholic claim, I was still bothered by the lack of unity among Christians, clearly against Christ's and Paul's commands. I investigated where we got the books of the Bible, as well as moral issues like the use of contraception, something I had always assumed was a good thing.

I began to be convinced as each belief I held that contradicted the Catholic Church's teaching had a reasonable answer to it, often more reasonable and biblical than my own belief's support. I learned about why the Catholic Church said contraception was immoral. I challenged my Evangelical friends with the arguments, which to them must have felt like a bolt of lightning out of the clear blue sky, and they failed to respond with convincing answers.

I remember the day I could see that the Catholic Church's claim *just might be true*. It was like the day when I, still an atheist, began to believe that Jesus Christ might really be whom He said He was. It was exhilarating! It meant that God had not left us alone to wallow in the corruption of error that plagued every heart and every institution. It meant that I could actually become holy! Though "all" sinned and fell short of God's glory, Jesus did not; this meant that we, too, could live in true freedom from the slavery of sin. Similarly, though "all" institutions, including churches, seem corrupt, the Church that Christ built Himself did not teach error because *Christ preserved her from it*. Even though she was and is made up of sinful human beings, God gave us the gift of His Church so that we could know the truth, be set free by it, and live the truth by the power of the Holy Spirit.

If Protestantism is true, then the Church is really no more reliable than any other human institution. Just as other groups of people can go far astray, so can the Church Christ founded. Any confidence put into His Church, then, is shaky; we must always take our stands with one foot out the door. Also, the people deemed "heretics" by the Church over the centuries and whose teachings were rejected as false might actually be right, since the Church, not being protected by God, might very well have erred on these decisions as well.

"The Catholic Church Prevented Vernacular Translations of the Bible"

A common Protestant misconception is that the Catholic Church deliberately kept the Bible in Latin and disallowed translations into other languages, because the Church wanted to keep control over the people and knew that once lay Christians could read the Bible for themselves, they would see all the false teachings the Church had added onto the Bible. "Fortunately," one might claim, "Martin Luther broke the Church of Rome's power by translating the Bible into German so that lay Christians could liberate themselves by rediscovering the biblical truths over Rome's lies."

Many hear this claim and implicitly accept it as true, but it is historically false. Firstly, Luther's translation of the Bible into German was not the first one. There were many Catholic translations leading up to the fifteenth century, long before Luther's New Testament translation in 1522. In fact, in the first 500 years of the Church's history, the Bible was translated into Old Latin, Egyptian (Coptic), Ethiopic, Gothic, Armenian, Georgian, and Syriac, with several additional translations into different dialects of those languages as well. Additionally, around the year 400 Jerome translated the Bible into the common Latin tongue.[4] If the Church had wanted to suppress the Bible from the common people, Latin would have been the *one* language to avoid.

In the 800s, Cyril and Methodius made translations of the liturgy and of the Bible for the Slavic peoples. Pope Benedict dedicated a Wednesday audience to these two saints' lives and described an interesting heresy that arose in their day:

> On the way they [Sts. Cyril and Methodius] stopped in Venice, where they had a heated discussion with the champions of the so-called "trilingual heresy" who claimed that there were only three languages in which it was lawful to praise God: Hebrew, Greek and Latin. The two brothers obviously forcefully opposed this claim. In Rome Cyril and Methodius were received by Pope Adrian II who led a procession to meet them....The Pope had also realized the great importance of their exceptional mission....Thus he did not hesitate to approve the mission of the two brothers in Great Moravia, accepting and approving the use of the Slavonic language in the liturgy. The Slavonic Books were laid on the altar...and the liturgy in the Slavonic tongue was celebrated in the Basilicas of St Peter, St Andrew and St Paul.[5]

If the Catholic Church were intent on controlling her members by restricting the language of the Bible and the liturgy, the trilingual heresy would have served her well, preventing all but the most educated from reading the Bible for themselves and restricting commoners to full reliance on the Church's priests and scholars. But since the Church did not and does not have this diabolical design, she rightly condemned this teaching for what it was, a heresy, and approved these saints' vernacular translation.

A second important point to consider is that, for all of the Church's history, she has been composed of people from all over the world, and these people have spoken different languages. It was therefore necessary to have a common language whereby lay Christians, scholars, monks, and theologians in every country could converse and understand one another concerning biblical passages and theological ideas like the Trinity. The Latin Vulgate became this *lingua franca* for most of Christian history, which is why Jerome's translation was so important.

Thirdly, it must be kept in mind that, especially before the printing press, literacy rates within Christendom were not nearly as high as they are today. The Church could not hope to communicate the gospel of Christ by telling everyone to "go home and read the Bible." All books—including the Bible—were painstakingly copied by hand (in the case of the Bible, by Catholic monks) and thus were rare and expensive. Instead, the Church read from the Bible during the liturgy, created works of art to publicly convey scenes from the Bible and Christ's life, and used other methods to teach the saving truths of the Faith to the lay people, whatever their education and material means.

A Protestant might object that though these examples may be accurate, it is still true that Luther and the other Reformers liberated interpretation of the Bible from the monopoly that the Catholic Church had held by making translations available to more Christians and empowering their personal interpretation of it.

While it is true that Luther at first thought that the German people would interpret the Bible the same way that he did (which he saw as the "clear" interpretation), he was quickly disabused of that notion. Protestant historian Alister McGrath describes the turnabout that Luther and Calvin took on the idea that the common man could understand the Bible:

> The magisterial Reformation initially seems to have allowed that every individual had the right to interpret Scripture; but....the Peasant's Revolt of 1525 appears to have convinced some, such as Luther, that individual believers (especially German peasants) were simply not capable of interpreting Scripture. It is one of the ironies of the Lutheran Reformation that a movement which laid such stress upon the importance of Scripture should subsequently deny its less educated members direct access to that same Scripture, for fear that they might misinterpret it (in other words, reach a different interpretation from that of the magisterial Reformers)....The direct interpretation of Scripture was thus effectively reserved for a small, privileged group of people. To put it crudely, it became a question of whether you looked to the pope, to Luther or to Calvin as an interpreter of Scripture. The principle of the "clarity of Scripture" appears to have been quietly marginalized, in the light of the use made of the Bible by the more radical elements [that is, the Anabaptists] of the Reformation.[6]

If Protestantism is true, then the Catholic Church did not want lay Christians to be able to read the Bible, so that she could keep them ignorant of the "true" interpretations of the Scriptures and thus retain power over them. Oddly, this same power-hungry Catholic Church sought to communicate the gospel to all people using every means possible, including music, art, architecture, the common tongue, and vernacular translations.

"The Catholic Church Puts God in a Box"

Protestants often charge the Catholic Church with "putting God in a box" by defining so many doctrines and dogmas: "God is bigger than doctrines and cannot be rigidly defined; Jesus refused to fit into people's expectations of Him and continually astounded them with His words and actions, demonstrating that they only *thought* they knew everything about God. The Catholic Church is the mod-

ern-day version of the scribes and Pharisees with their human traditions and legalistic enforcement of hundreds of little laws."

Is it really applying limits to God when we pronounce His doctrine? The Catholic Church does not proactively go out her way to
define every corner of the Faith with a doctrinal statement. Instead,
she very selectively and minimally states things to be true, and these
only when she needs to do so.

We do not understand everything perfectly. Even the dogma of
the Trinity only gives us a glimpse into the incomprehensibly beautiful divine exchange of love among the Persons of the Trinity,
something we will only see in the Beatific Vision after we have died
in Christ's mercy. The dogma that Christ is really present in the Eucharist similarly can tell us that Jesus is present in the consecrated
host and that we receive Him there (body, blood, soul, and divinity),
but it cannot plumb the depths of wonder and grace that God
pours into our souls when He comes to us so humbly in holy communion. The "box" that many Protestants perceive is more like an
arrow that points to the infinite mystery Who is our Lord, and
truthful doctrines ensure that the arrow points in the right direction.

If Protestantism is true, then binding doctrines can never be established by Protestant communities, otherwise they would be acting
like the Catholic Church in her proclamation of dogmas, which
Protestants claim is confining to God and unbiblical.

"The Catholic Church Does Not Produce Good Fruit"

Jesus said that "a tree is known by its fruit" (Matt. 12:33), so one
way we can determine whether people are true Christians is to look
for good fruit in their lives. Many Protestants claim that they know
the Catholic Church and her teachings are false because "the
Church does not produce good fruit."

How can they tell? Well, a typical Protestant church has at least a
few ex-Catholics, and most of these Catholics were very poorly
formed in their Faith, if they received any formation at all. Sadly,
many of these Catholics even went to Catholic schools for much of
their life and were raised by (at least nominally) Catholic parents.
When asked basic questions about God and the Faith, they have no
clue how to answer. Unsurprisingly, sometime shortly after high

school, when their parents could no longer force them to go to Mass on Sundays, they dropped out and eventually abandoned the practice of their faith entirely. Then, a trial or crisis hits, and a faithful Protestant Christian shares with them the basics of the gospel—which they *should* have received long ago. By God's grace, they believe in it and begin living their faith. They go to the particular Protestant church of the person who evangelized them, start reading the Bible (which they have never read before), and "come alive in Christ."

Their lives are transformed as they grow in their faith and love of God. They look back at their life growing up as a Catholic and quickly come to believe from talking with their new Protestant brethren that they were taught a bunch of false, man-made traditions instead of the "biblical truth." They never read their Bible growing up because no one in their family did; they zoned out during Mass, so they never heard the Scriptures there, either. Now, however, they believe in Jesus and have a relationship with Him. They read their Bible and grow in knowledge of God and also are reaffirmed in the specific Protestant beliefs they have begun accepting. They are grateful that they "were saved out of the false Roman Catholic religion."

Is it any wonder, then, that Protestants and these former Catholics think poorly of the Catholic Church? The natural conclusion that they draw is that the Catholic religious system leads to death and not to the life that Christ gives. Therefore, all the reasons in the world cannot overcome the belief that the "Roman Church" leads people away from the gospel rather than to it.

Although I would never question the joy and celebration of such a person's newfound friendship with God, or the tragic and valid complaints of their poor religious training, such experiences don't actually *prove* a lack of good fruit but more accurately a lack of good "gardening." If we accept as evidence the most unfortunate examples of Catholics who fall away from the Church, we should also admit the best examples that the Catholic Faith engenders. How does a moribund Church of merely human traditions produce someone like Mother Teresa of Calcutta, who dedicated her life to serving the poorest of the poor in India, people abandoned by everyone and literally dying in filth in the streets of the cities? How do we explain her rationale that in every one of these grungy, sickened persons, she saw the suffering face of Jesus Christ? These teachings come straight from the Bible, and the Catholic Church proclaims them loudly: "Whatever you did for one of the least of these brothers of mine, you did for me" (Matt. 25:40). Mother Teresa was taught authentic, orthodox Catholicism, rather than the anemic form so often received by those persons nominally reared in the Catholic Church. When the true Catholic Faith is taught and lived out, people are transformed by God's grace and become vibrant, Christ-centered men and women of the kingdom.

Mother Teresa is just one example of a Catholic who bore good fruit and who demonstrated that she had the life of Christ within her. There are millions upon millions more in whom God's light has shown, the most famous of which are the saints. Reading their lives is inspiring and challenging, akin to reading about Paul's courageous and unswerving devotion to Jesus. And all of these saints were faithful Catholics to the core. They wrote with eloquence and unshakable faith about the sacraments, the Church's Tradition, the Scriptures, the obedience due to the bishops as the Apostles' successors, and the primacy of the bishop of Rome, Peter's successor.

Within the Catholic Church, both weeds and wheat are growing up together, just as Jesus promised (see Matt. 13:24–30), and only at the time of the harvest will the angels separate them.

If Protestantism is true, then the Catholic Church is false, because her members do not bear good fruit. Yet, Catholic nuns and religious orders are serving the poor in India, running hospices for AIDS patients in Africa, and fighting for the rights of the impoverished and downtrodden all over the world. Catholic maternity homes provide safe places for young women who are pregnant and afraid, truly giving them the choice to keep their babies instead of aborting them. Catholic universities and schools have existed for hundreds of years to form the entire human person, both intellectually and spiritually. Catholics give millions of dollars in charity every year to a vast number of organizations that provide material and spiritual aid for those in need. And Catholics in the public sphere fight for the dignity of all human life from conception to natural death, for traditional marriage, and for the prioritization of the human person over the almighty dollar in the economy. Finally,

Catholics the world over love God and spread the gospel of Jesus Christ, sharing His love and truth with others.

"The Early Church Was Like Protestantism"

Protestants assert that in the early centuries of the Church, she was comprised of many loosely connected churches, largely autonomous and often in disagreement with one another—much like Protestantism today—and that these individual churches together made up the Church; there was no one person who acted as the head of the Church nor any visible unity in doctrine or hierarchy.

To respond to this argument, let's recall some facts about the Church throughout history, beginning with the first centuries. If this claim were true, how does one explain the ecumenical council of Nicaea, where the Church's bishops met to determine whether Arianism was a heresy or not? The leaders of the visible Church met to authoritatively decide whether Arius's teachings were orthodox, and the Church decided unequivocally that they were heterodox, drawing up the Nicene Creed in response and demanding that all of the bishops proclaim this same Creed or be declared heretics. This decision was binding upon all Christians, and anyone who rejected it could be excommunicated from the Church.

Ignatius of Antioch in the early 100s cautioned Christians to avoid the heretical schisms that had broken off from the Church: "But flee from all abominable heresies, and those that cause schisms."[7] His words underscore the reality of the Church's visible unity in spite of the schisms that had already arisen. Irenaeus wrote later in the second century that

> the Church, spread throughout the whole world, carefully guards the faith and preaching it has received, as though living in one and the same house; and its faith is the same in every place, as if the Church had one soul and heart, and whatever it preaches, teaches and transmits, it does so in unison, as if from one mouth.[8]

These two early Christian leaders, both bishops, demonstrate that the early Church was not a loose collection of independent churches that each taught their own set of doctrines without regard to a hierarchical authority. If the Church had operated as Protestants claim that she did, what we should see in history are hundreds of competing groups teaching and believing their own things, sending no bishops to any type of authoritative council to decide universally on whether something was true or false but rather each coming up with their own interpretation of the Bible. But we do not see that, not until the Protestant Reformation of the 1500s when the Protestant churches, having rejected the unifying principle of Christ's Church, began operating under this new idea of what the Church is.

If Protestantism is true, then the Church throughout all of history has operated under the current Protestant model of local congregations and denominational families, each contradicting one another on many important doctrines but all lacking any authority to make binding decisions about truth and falsehood. No councils or authoritative decrees could have been made by the Church, for that would suggest a central authority.

Inexplicably, however, this loose confederation of conflicting groups was *at the same time* the visible, hierarchically organized, historical Church that convened councils and made binding decisions about the content of divine revelation.

"The Catholic Church Invented Doctrines Late in History"

Some Protestants contend that the Catholic Church throughout her history has aggressively defined hundreds or even thousands of doctrines—some of them only very recently—even though many of these doctrines are not found in the Bible. They argue that the Catholic Church has used these doctrines to further her agenda.

The truth is the opposite. The Catholic Church has tremendous respect for the mystery of God and His truth, a mystery that here on this earth can only be glimpsed at. In particular, she is extremely conservative when it comes to declaring something as true about God. In fact, throughout history it is most often the case that the Church is forced to define the boundaries of truth because they are challenged by someone who teaches heresy as truth. So it is in a defensive posture that the Church works with regard to formulating doctrine. She does not proclaim in an exhaustive way every single thing that is true about God—as if that were possible for us finite creatures—but rather proclaims that, whatever you may want to believe about God, there are certain things that are *not* true and so should not be believed, and there are a few things that are certainly true (though perhaps still mysterious) which must be believed.

Though a particular teaching may only be declared as true *dogmatically* at some late date, that belief has always been true, and there is always evidence of it being believed in the history of the Church. For example, the Immaculate Conception of the Virgin Mary was dogmatically decreed in the year 1854, but when you read the Fathers of the Church—popes, bishops, faithful kings, monks, etc.— down through the centuries, you hear them speaking of the immaculate Mother of God over and over again. You even see great works of art devoted to Mary Immaculate centuries before this teaching was declared dogmatically.

The gift of infallibility to the Church is a *negative* protection, that is, a protection against teaching error, rather than a command that the pope and the Church will always proactively teach every possible thing that is true about God and the Faith. That list would be inexhaustible because God himself, the Source of all truth, can never be fully described by us creatures through any set of teachings. Rather, God protects the Church from teaching error as truth. She is the servant of the Truth, not its master.

If Protestantism is true, then the Catholic Church has continually invented false, man-made doctrines, in which no Christian should have to believe, and has done so for centuries. Yet Protestants agree with the Church's decisions on the fundamental doctrines about the nature of God and the New Testament canon of Scripture. On these matters—settled centuries after Christ died and rose— Protestants accede willingly and make no claim that they were novelties. So what criteria do Protestants use to determine which decisions of the Church had divine origin and which were man-made? That's a good question.

Chapter Eight
The Sacraments

Brent had spent time in many different Christian churches. He grew up in the churches of Christ but later left that denomination and drifted for a while. After he married, he and his wife went to a Quaker meeting, one that was "unprogrammed," which meant they had no pastor or structure for their weekly service. Instead, everyone sat in silence until someone felt led by the Holy Spirit to share an insight with the others.

I got to know Brent on a professional level and collaborated with him for many years at work, but only after I married did we begin a friendship outside of our jobs. Brent and his wife, Alicia, were a quiet, reflective couple, drawn to tightly knit communities like the Mennonites (and also sympathetic to the idea of pacifism).

One evening we went on a double date, and they told us about an experience they had had on their recent trip to Italy. They were visiting the Sanctuary of St. Francis at Chiusi della Verna when they both felt a deeply peaceful, maternal presence around them. It lasted for a short time and then passed. Intuitively they knew it was the Virgin Mary. Since neither one of them had grown up with any kind of Marian devotion, this experience was even more extraordinary.

This event motivated Brent to ask questions about my Catholic faith. At first, our discussion focused on baptism, as the founder of the Quakers eschewed water baptism, pointing out that many people had been baptized yet continued to lead immoral lives. The Quaker view bothered Brent, as his baptism in the churches of Christ had had a profound impact on him. I pointed out the Catholic arguments for water baptism, including some of the ones in this chapter, and that led to many lively conversations about how the sacraments work and whether God instituted them. One sticking point for him was the fact that the Catholic Church practiced "closed communion," meaning only Catholics could receive the Eucharist.

In spite of our differences, our conversation continued to make progress. Brent and Alicia were both accomplished musicians of classical music and deeply appreciated the contributions that Catholic composers had made to their field. Their concerts were often held in an old Catholic cathedral, which increased their respect for the Church's architecture and liturgy.

But the leap from Quaker to Catholic proved to be too much. One practical and a few theological obstacles stood in their way. Still, they knew that they could not remain Quaker, so they joined an Episcopal church in their area and began regularly attending services there. People often joke that the Episcopal Church is "Catholic lite," and while I don't view it as such, it is true that its liturgy resembles the Catholic Church's, as does its hierarchical structure.

Brent and I continued our discussions, focusing on the two most important issues in his mind: the papacy (including papal infallibility) and whether Christ established a visible Church or not. I encouraged him to read the writings of the early Christians on these topics, and he did this and more, studying books about the Church's history in addition to the works of the Church Fathers. The primary obstacle for Brent at this point is the need for more faith. Arguments and reasons—however well founded—can only take you so far. Their purpose is to provide support for making the assent of faith in Christ and His Church, and this is the last step Brent needs to take.

He is still considering the arguments and praying about becoming Catholic. The practical obstacle preventing him from entering full communion with the Church has been resolved, another positive consequence from our dialogue. He and I continue our friendship, and I continue to pray for him, for the grace and courage to follow where God leads.

The Sacraments

The Catholic and the Orthodox Churches recognize seven sacraments: baptism, confirmation, holy communion (or the Eucharist), confession (also called penance or reconciliation), anointing of the sick, marriage, and holy orders. The sacraments are divinely instituted signs through which God also gives grace to the persons receiving them. In baptism, for example, water is poured over a person (or she is immersed) while the minister invokes the name of the Holy Trinity; this sacrament symbolizes being buried in death with Christ and then rising with Him. Through this act, God communicates the grace of being washed clean of sin. The Holy Spirit comes to dwell within the new Christian, and she becomes a member of Christ's mystical Body, the Church. These effects of baptism are summarized by the phrase "baptismal regeneration."

Are the sacraments necessary for salvation? Yes, ordinarily they are, but God is not limited by the sacraments He instituted, so that "savage in Africa" so often pictured, who has never heard of Jesus or received any sacraments, can still be saved by God's great mercy. The thief on the cross was saved similarly. The sacraments are the *ordinary* way that God communicates His grace to people and assures them of His saving actions, but they are not the only ways that God gives grace.

Protestants know quite well that they have received God's grace apart from full communion with the Catholic Church, and any Catholic denying this fact not only argues against the Church but against Christ Himself: "For everyone who asks receives; the one who seeks finds; and to the one who knocks, the door will be opened. Which of you fathers, if your son asks for a fish, will give him a snake instead? . . . how much more will your Father in heaven give the Holy Spirit to those who ask him!" (Luke 11:10–11, 13b NIV). And so I emphasize here again that Protestants are our dearly loved brothers and sisters in the family of God, on whom God pours out His grace and care. However, they are in error about the sacraments.

Though some sacraments are spoken of more frequently than others in the Scriptures, evidence for all seven of the sacraments is found in the Bible. Nonetheless, Protestantism, following the lead set by Martin Luther, rejects all the sacraments except for baptism and holy communion. Even so, the term "sacrament" is usually avoided in favor or "ordinance" or something else. In this chapter, we will explore why Luther, Calvin, and then Protestantism in general rejected most of the sacraments and examine whether this decision holds up biblically, historically, and theologically.

The Unanimous Teaching of Baptismal Regeneration

The Church has taught the doctrine of baptismal regeneration from the beginning of her existence. This doctrine holds that people are regenerated, justified, and united to Christ through baptism. The Holy Spirit comes to dwell within them, and they are then said to be in a state of sanctifying grace (friendship with God). The witness of the early Christians' writings and those of the Church Fathers are universally in support of this understanding. Around the year 150, Justin Martyr wrote, that

> As many as are persuaded and believe that what we [Christians] teach and say is true, and undertake to be able to live accordingly...are brought by us where there is water, and are regenerated in the same manner in which we were ourselves regenerated. For, in the name of God, the Father and Lord of the universe, and of our Savior Jesus Christ, and of the Holy Spirit, they then receive the washing with water. For Christ also said, "Except you be born again, you shall not enter into the kingdom of heaven." [1]

Justin is referencing a passage from John's gospel where Jesus is speaking to Nicodemus:

> Jesus answered him, "Truly, truly, I say to you, unless one is born anew, he cannot see the kingdom of God." Nicodemus said to him, "How can a man be born when he is old? Can he enter a second time into his mother's womb and be born?" Jesus answered, "Truly, truly, I say to you, unless one is born of water and the Spirit, he cannot enter the kingdom of God" (John 3:3–5).

Justin explains that Jesus is talking about baptism in this passage. If, however, you ask a Protestant today what these verses mean, you will hear many different answers, few of which will connect it with baptism, since Protestants in general reject the doctrine of baptismal regeneration, in spite of the testimony of the early Christians.

In the third century, Tertullian, Hippolytus, and Origen lent further evidence to baptismal regeneration with their writings. Baptism is also explicitly mentioned in the Nicene Creed: "We confess one baptism for the forgiveness of sins." Interestingly, the Nicene Creed is affirmed not only by the Catholic and Orthodox Churches, but also by most Protestant communities. Yet, Protestants do not believe that God forgives sins through baptism! So Protestant Christians are left in the inconsistent position of having to affirm this ancient, universally accepted creed while simultaneously performing a double-think when they proclaim the words "one baptism for the forgiveness of sins," interpreting them to mean something like "one baptism for the symbolic, outward proclamation that one has put his faith in Jesus."

Baptism, *Sola Fide*, and Salvation: Two Different Understandings

Though Protestants retained baptism as something that every Christian should do, they disagree about what God does or does not do through baptism and whether or not it is connected with one's salvation. Protestants, following John Calvin, flatly reject the Catholic Church's teaching on baptismal regeneration; however, Martin Luther's beliefs about this sacrament were quite close to Catholicism's and therefore much more sacramental than those of the other Reformers.

For many Protestants, especially Evangelicals, baptism is something that *they* do for God. It's a stand they take, a message they send to their church and to society. They make a decision to give their life to Jesus, and they get baptized to demonstrate outwardly to the church what Jesus has already done in them inwardly. They believe that God gives no grace through baptism; rather, they believe that they already received the Holy Spirit when they asked Jesus into their hearts and put their faith in Him as their Lord and Savior. All of the important things, the ones that Protestants believe are necessary for salvation, have thus been completed, so by getting baptized, they are simply demonstrating their obedience to Jesus and making a public proclamation of their faith in Him for all to see.

Under this paradigm, how is baptism connected to faith and salvation? Why participate in this messy symbolic action at all? Let's look to John Calvin for the standard Protestant answer to that question. Calvin, following Luther, taught that faith alone justifies, *sola fide*, and both taught that a person received salvation as a gift from God by putting their faith in Jesus's promises as recorded in the gospels. Fair enough. But now an important difference emerges between these two most important Protestant Reformers: Which of Jesus's promises, exactly, is the one considered the most fundamental?

For Calvin, the promise was from Mark 16:16: "Whoever believes...will be saved." So, it logically follows that, *if* I believe in Christ, *then* I will be saved, for God has promised it. Since I know that I believe, I can conclude that Christ's promise applies to me and so can say "I am saved." This belief is called "faith alone" because the promise of salvation that Jesus makes to me depends only upon my faith.

Anglican Protestant theologian Phillip Cary further develops this idea:

> How do I get saved? Well, by believing, of course. This is an explicit condition of the promise....So the logic follows from this condition: you are saved on condition that you have faith, so if I am to know I am saved I must know I meet the condition. Indeed, because the content of the promise is conditional, explicitly making everything conditional upon faith, I am in no position to say the gospel promise is about me until I can say, "I believe." For most Protestants, this is a really big deal. The hour I first believed, the moment when I can first say "I truly believe in Christ" is the moment of my salvation, of my conversion and turning from death to life. What matters is that moment of conversion, not the sacrament of baptism, because everything depends on my being able to say "I believe." For only if I know that I truly believe can I confidently conclude: I am saved. Notice what this requires of us: not just that we believe, but that we *know* we believe.[2]

Martin Luther (and the Catholic Church), on the other hand, taught a sacramental understanding of baptism, that it is something that *God* does for *you*. So a person places his faith in Jesus Christ, Who baptized him and made promises to him through this sacrament. Jesus's command to His Apostles to baptize in Matthew 28 was seen by Luther as the fundamental promise. Therefore it is Jesus Christ Himself who, through the minister of baptism, speaks the words "I baptize you in the name of the Father, and of the Son, and of the Holy Spirit," and baptizes the person. This was Luther's teaching, and it is also the teaching of the Catholic Church, reaffirmed in the document *Sacrosanctum Concilium* in the Second Vatican Council. Alister McGrath confirms that "for Luther, baptism was the cause of faith."[3]

Luther's belief about baptism's connection to faith would surprise most Protestants. Dr. Phillip Cary describes the nature of this connection:

> This is why for Luther Christian faith is quite literally faith in one's baptism. To have faith in Christ is to believe him when he says, "I baptize you" in the name of the Father, the Son and the Holy Spirit." Since baptism signifies new life in Christ, faith justifies us by receiving this new life. Faith in effect speaks thus: Christ says he baptizes me, and therefore (since baptism means new life in Christ) I have new life in Christ. Hence for Luther justification does not require us to have a conversion experience or make a decision for Christ. These are acts of will that would detract from Luther's point about faith alone: that we are justified merely by believing what Christ says is true. The logical connection is made by Luther's motto, "believe it and you have it": to believe in your baptism is to have the new life Christ signifies when he baptizes you.[4]

Martin Luther himself defended his belief on *sola fide* and baptism against other Protestant groups that claimed baptism was merely an external, symbolic act:

But as our would-be wise, new spirits assert that faith alone saves, and that works and external things avail nothing, we answer: it is true, indeed, that nothing in us is of any avail but faith, as we shall hear still further. But these blind guides are unwilling to see this, namely, that faith must have something which it believes, that is, of which it takes hold, and upon which it stands and rests. Thus faith clings to the water, and believes that it is Baptism, in which there is pure salvation and life; not through the water (as we have sufficiently stated), but through the fact that it is embodied in the Word and institution of God, and the name of God inheres in it.[5]

For Catholics and Martin Luther, baptism is all about what Christ does for us and not what we do for Christ. We do not have to know that we have faith or to "have faith in our faith," but rather, we accept the promise of Jesus which He applies to us when He baptizes us. Our faith is in Jesus's action, and in times where we doubt or have uncertainty about the quality of our faith or love of God, we can look back at the promise Christ made to us at the place and time when we were baptized.[6]

Given this subtle yet deep difference between Calvin and Luther, a reasonable question to ask is: "Why should we believe Calvin over Luther on this matter?" Luther's beliefs here were much more in line with the unchanging teaching on baptism of the Church since the first century. Ironically, it was Luther himself who undermined his chances of winning all of Protestantism over to his teachings on this issue. By rejecting five sacraments outright and modifying the doctrine of how Christ is present in the Eucharist, he demonstrated no scruples in altering or removing six of the seven sacraments. Is it unreasonable then for another Protestant leader to change the meaning of the seventh one as well? If the sacraments were "fair game" and the Catholic Church erred for centuries on six of them, what are the odds that she didn't also get the seventh one wrong in a fundamental way, as Calvin and his followers argued?

The spirit of Protestantism is one that allows any Christian to challenge Church teachings, no matter how ancient and well-attested they may be. We could say that Luther paved this road himself but was then run over on it by his fellow Protestants. Even his fundamental doctrine of "faith alone" was understood in a *substantially* different way by the second most influential Protestant Reformer.

Infant Baptism

Should infants be baptized? That simple question has plagued the different movements within Protestantism since its beginning and continues to be a divisive issue among them. At the heart of the dispute is the difference in Protestant understandings of what *sola Scriptura* means with regard to the place of *tradition* in Christian doctrine. The unchanging teaching and practice of the Catholic Church, as well as of all the Orthodox Churches, is to baptize infants. Interestingly, Martin Luther again proves an unexpected ally to the Catholic Church on this issue, as his beliefs on infant baptism and the reasons for it are quite Catholic.

Recall from the previous section that Luther believed that God communicated grace to the person being baptized and that it was God Himself who baptized through the minister. Luther also recognized that the Church had always baptized infants, up to and including the sixteenth century when he began the Reformation. Combining this universal practice of the Church with his sacramental understanding of baptism, "Luther regarded infant baptism as the means by which God brought about faith in individuals."[7]

In other words, God bestowed the theological virtue of faith on the individual through the sacrament of baptism. Luther offered an eminently reasonable explanation of how we can know that infant baptism is pleasing to God:

> But if God did not accept the baptism of infants, He would not give the Holy Ghost nor any of His gifts to any of them; in short, during this long time unto this day no man upon earth could have been a Christian. Now, since God confirms Baptism by the gifts of His Holy Ghost as is plainly perceptible in some of the church fathers, as St. Bernard…and others, who were baptized in infancy, and since the holy Christian Church cannot perish until the end of the world, they must acknowledge that such infant baptism is pleasing to God.[8]

His reasoning is compelling: if infant baptism is invalid, then since the vast majority of Christians were baptized as infants, they were invalidly baptized and thus never received the Holy Spirit or the virtues of faith, hope, and love. They were therefore not members of Christ's Church and thus could not even be rightfully called Christians, a preposterous idea contradicted by the many saints who demonstrated their love of God and neighbor in their lives of heroic virtue.

The Anabaptists (literally, "rebaptizers") were the radical movement within the Reformation. They rebaptized anyone who followed them, because they rejected infant baptism as invalid, instead claiming that the Bible clearly taught credo-baptism ("believer's baptism"). To them, *sola Scriptura* meant that every doctrine should be explicitly found in the Bible without the influence of traditions, even those of the early Church as found in the writings of the Councils, the Fathers, and other early Christians. If a doctrine was not explicitly stated in the Bible itself, then it was not to be taught as true, and they rightly pointed out that nowhere in the New Testament does it explicitly say that an infant is baptized.

The Anabaptists went further, however, and asserted that the doctrines of the Trinity and of the divinity of Christ were also not explicitly found in Scripture and thus should not be accepted. These incredible claims were based on the belief that the Bible could be accurately interpreted by any Christian who had the Holy Spirit and that an individual's judgment could trump that of the Church.

The magisterial Reformers—Luther, Zwingli, and Calvin—were appalled by the Radical Reformers' rejection of even the most sacred of Christian teachings. For them, it was good and even necessary to look to the traditions of the early Church and to the writings of the Church Fathers—especially those of Augustine—in order to formulate true doctrines. The magisterial Reformers believed that these great saints had (for the most part) developed sound biblical theology by correctly interpreting the Scriptures. The errors they saw in the Fathers' teachings would of course be corrected by their own, wiser understanding of theology, but the core doctrines were to be preserved insofar as they were in harmony with Scripture.

And the Trinity, the divinity of Christ, and infant baptism were most certainly in harmony with the Bible.

Protestantism today has inherited this centuries-old division from its founding fathers. The situation is even more dizzying given the vast number of Protestant splits that have occurred since the 1500s. Most Protestant traditions baptize infants, but large groups of Protestants, especially Baptists, most other Evangelical Protestants, and the very populous Pentecostal communities, reject it as unbiblical.

The irreconcilable Protestant beliefs on infant baptism present a dilemma for any Bible-believing Protestant today. Either the magisterial Reformers were correct in teaching that infant baptism was true, in spite of the fact that it nowhere appears in Scripture explicitly, or the Radical Reformers were correct in rejecting infant baptism as an unbiblical practice on which the Church had fallen into error from the beginning.

Yet to accept the Radical Reformers' interpretation would trust them as having a credible claim to faithful Scriptural interpretation, something hard to concede given the fact that the Anabaptists also rejected the Trinity and Christ's divinity as unbiblical. (These rejections are quite rare today, though the Oneness Pentecostals are known for their anti-Trinitarian stance.) The problem with accepting the magisterial Reformers' acceptance of the ancient tradition of infant baptism lies in the fact that doing so raises a thorny question: if we accept this particular tradition of the early Church, even though it is nowhere defined in the Bible, on what basis do we reject other ancient traditions like prayers for the dead, the Mass, purgatory, the primacy of the church of Rome, and baptismal regeneration—all of which have as much or even more scriptural support as does infant baptism?

Protestants embrace *sola Scriptura*, but they have yet to agree on whether *sola Scriptura* also includes room for the influence of Christian tradition and noncanonical early works. Only after this matter is settled can one make a judgment on the validity of infant baptism.

The Protestant Rejection of Marriage as a Sacrament

The Catholic Church teaches that "sacraments are outward signs of inward grace, instituted by Christ for our sanctification."[9] We have seen that Protestants, following the lead of Martin Luther, explicitly rejected five of the seven sacraments, including marriage. However, as will be demonstrated, Protestants in reality believe that marriage is an outward sign of inward grace, so their rejection of marriage as a "sacrament" has apparently dissolved.

Genesis 2:24 says, "That is why a man leaves his father and mother and clings to his wife, and the two of them become one flesh." In Mark 10, Jesus reaffirms this teaching on marriage in explaining why divorce is impossible. From these verses and the universal witness of Christian history, clearly marriage is something instituted by God and pleasing to Him. A Christian man and woman have a wedding ceremony where they exchange marriage vows. Then they consummate their vows through the marital embrace, and in doing so, they become one flesh. God joins them together as one, and even if they get a civil divorce certificate from the State, in God's eyes, and therefore in reality, they are still married.

Thus, the sacrament of marriage is an *outward sign*—the wedding ceremony, the dress, the rings, the bells, the procession, the vows, and the marital embrace—which signify the very real *inward grace* that God gives, joining them as one flesh. We know that the joining of the two as one flesh, while outwardly accomplished through sexual intercourse, must also be an inward action that God performs, for when two people marry, they do not become physically conjoined together as one inseparable person. They appear as two distinct persons, walking around and going off in different directions every day. And to all outward appearances, there is no reason why they each could not choose another person, have a wedding ceremony, and then have relations with that new person instead. We as Christians would call that adultery, for the very reason that God Himself joined the first two people together in the one-flesh union.

So we see that all Christians believe in the Bible's clear teaching that in marriage, God works an inward grace in the two persons that joins them together. This is the definition of a sacrament. Therefore, since Protestants believe that God gives inward grace through outward actions in marriage, even if they don't call it a "sacrament," what is the principled reason for denying that He does the same thing through other sacraments?

Anointing of the Sick

The anointing of the sick is one of the seven sacraments in the Catholic and Orthodox Churches. It is also sometimes known as extreme unction or last rites (though it is not just reserved for Christians on their deathbed). In this sacrament, the priest or bishop anoints the sick person with blessed oil and prays over her for the Holy Spirit to heal her body and soul. If it is best for her salvation, the anointed person is healed of her illness, but regardless of whether the Lord chooses to heal her physically, He bestows grace on her and forgives her sins, in accordance with the Scriptures: "Is anyone among you sick? He should summon the presbyters of the church, and they should pray over him and anoint (him) with oil in the name of the Lord, and the prayer of faith will save the sick person, and the Lord will raise him up. If he has committed any sins, he will be forgiven" (James 5:14–15).

The Gospel of Mark also speaks of Christ sending the Apostles out to heal people by anointing them with oil: "They drove out many demons, and they anointed with oil many who were sick and cured them" (Mark 6:13). The biblical witness and the historical practice of the Church from the earliest centuries in both East and West confirm that this sacrament was apostolic and instituted by Christ. Yet the Protestant Reformers rejected it, and all of Protestantism followed after them.[10] Why?

Martin Luther was first in rejecting it, providing a litany of reasons for why he did so. His strongest argument against the sacrament was that, since people who received it during his day were on their deathbed and most did not recover from their illness, it was not a true sacrament. The error he made was in assuming that the person's physical recovery was the vital component of the anointing. Instead, the person's spiritual health—the state of his soul—was and is the primary purpose of this sacrament, especially for those persons who were soon to meet God (note Christ's priorities toward the seriously ill in Matthew 9:2–7). His other arguments include the rejection of the book of James altogether as uninspired and also—even when he assumes for the sake of argument that James is canonical—that an Apostle has no right to create a sacrament. He claims that the Gospels make no mention of it, ignoring or embarrassingly missing Mark 6:13.

John Calvin followed Luther in rejecting this sacrament, though he gave a different reason for doing so:

> But the gift of healing disappeared with the other miraculous powers which the Lord was pleased to give for a time, that it might render the new preaching of the gospel for ever wonderful. Therefore, even were we to grant that anointing was a sacrament of those powers which were then administered by the hands of the apostles, it pertains not to us, to whom no such powers have been committed.[11]

Calvin, ignoring the universal historical witness to the sacrament in the Church, rejects anointing of the sick out of hand because of his opinion that God no longer worked miracles through His ministers. This arbitrary, extra-biblical tradition is contrary to the sacred Scriptures and the Tradition of the Church. It is startling that one of the most influential men behind Protestantism so cavalierly dismissed one of the seven sacraments of the Christian Church, offering only his own opinion as rationale for doing so.

When I was an Evangelical Protestant going to a Southern Baptist church, my pastor gave a sermon where he recounted an experience he had had of being asked by a hospitalized church member to come and pray over him and anoint him with oil. The church member explicitly mentioned James 5 as the biblical precedent for the request. My pastor said, "Sure enough, I looked it up, and it's right there in the Bible just like he said. So I didn't really know what to do, but I went to the hospital and took some oil with me, and then, well, I *poped* him!" This last statement was accompanied by the pastor making the gesture of the sign of the Cross. Raucous laughter and applause from the congregation followed. I would have found it funny, too, had I not recently begun to consider that the Catholic Church's claim might be true and therefore that this sacrament being joked about might also be something ordained by God.

This Baptist church claims the Bible alone as the sole source of revelation and rule of faith, but my pastor had never done what James said he should do before, that is, pray over a sick parishioner and anoint him with oil. In fact, my pastor knew that this was something that only the *Catholics* did; perhaps he even knew that it was one of the seven sacraments of the Catholic Church. So faced with the Bible-based request, he turned to the experts on the matter. He did what the Catholic Church has done for 2,000 years: he made the sign of the Cross with the oil and prayed over the sick person.

The Eucharist

Infant baptism is one polarizing issue for Protestantism. The Eucharist is another. What did Jesus mean by "this is my body?" Catholics say that He really meant "this is my body" and that He transformed the bread and wine into His body and blood. Luther said that he meant "this is my body," but he rejected the philosophical underpinnings of the Catholic dogma of transubstantiation in favor of something called sacramental union (or "consubstantiation"), the idea that Jesus is present with or beside the bread and wine. Zwingli, the Swiss Reformer, broke from the Catholic Church and from Luther by declaring the novel idea that Jesus only meant that "this signifies my body." Zwingli thus held a symbolic view of the Eucharist, rejecting any notion of Jesus being present in the bread and wine. Calvin, as usual, tried to steer a path in between his two precursors, ultimately landing very close to Zwingli's symbolic view.

Luther and Zwingli met early on in their respective reformations to try to come to an agreement on the Eucharist. Neither would budge on what he believed to be true on this most important issue. They utterly failed to agree, to compromise, or to even find common ground on which to move forward with discussions. Luther trenchantly made the observation that if, when Jesus says "this is my body," He didn't in some real way mean "this is my body," then it is impossible for anyone to accurately interpret the Scriptures.

Since Luther taught the doctrine of the perspicuity (clearness) of the Scriptures, the error was not that the Bible was not clear but that others (like Zwingli) interpreted its clear words wrongly, while he interpreted them rightly.

Thus in the early decades of the Reformation, already irreconcilable differences existed between the leading Reformers. Each one presumed himself an authority and was thus unwilling to submit to the other's beliefs. Why *should* he? What authority did Zwingli (or Luther) have that another should accept his beliefs? The cornerstone of Protestantism was laid: every man is ultimately an authority unto himself.

What did the Church believe about the Eucharist in the early centuries? Reading the Church Fathers and other early Christians, it becomes clear that the Catholic dogma of the real presence of Jesus Christ in the Eucharist was the teaching then, as it is now. The purely symbolic belief in the Eucharist is found nowhere in early writings. Luther certainly knew this fact, being well-versed in the early Christians, which is no doubt one reason why his teaching of sacramental union was, at least on paper, very close to the Catholic Church's.

Ignatius of Antioch lived during the Apostolic age and died in the first decade of the 100s. He wrote against the Docetist heretics, who taught that Jesus only *appeared* to be a truly flesh-and-blood human being: "Take note of those who hold heterodox opinions on the grace of Jesus Christ which has come to us, and see how contrary their opinions are to the mind of God....They abstain from the Eucharist and from prayer because they do not confess that the Eucharist is the flesh of our Savior Jesus Christ, flesh which suffered for our sins and which that Father, in his goodness, raised up again. They who deny the gift of God are perishing in their disputes."[12]

In the second and third centuries, Justin Martyr, Irenaeus, Clement of Alexandria, Tertullian, Hippolytus, Origen, and Cyprian of Carthage all attested to the real presence of Christ in the Eucharist. Today, however, most Protestants unwittingly accept their beliefs on the Eucharist from the Reformers, oblivious to the universal witness in the early Church to the real presence.

Faithful and intelligent Protestants for centuries have read their Bibles and prayed and yet come to mutually exclusive conclusions as to whether Christ is present in the Eucharist and if so, how He is present. This issue is not a matter where we can just all agree to disagree. There is a teaching that is true, and the others are half-truths or even (well-intentioned) falsehoods. Which one is it? How do we know?

Confession

In the sacrament of confession, the repentant Christian confesses his sins to a priest, and the priest, acting in the person of Christ and with Christ's divine authority, forgives the penitent person. That person is thus forgiven of his sin by God and also reconciled to Christ's Church, which he wounded by committing sins. It must be understood aright that it is God who forgives sins, but, as in so many other ways, God chooses to work through human instruments to communicate His free gift of grace.

Biblical support for this teaching is found in John 20:21–23:

> (Jesus) said to them again, "Peace be with you. As the Father has sent me, so I send you." And when he had said this, he breathed on them and said to them, "Receive the Holy Spirit. Whose sins you forgive are forgiven them, and whose sins you retain are retained."

Christ was speaking here to the Apostles shortly after his Resurrection. Additionally, James 5:16 indicates that we are to confess our sins to one another so that we may be forgiven, a verse directly associated with the priestly anointing and absolution of sins given in the verses just prior about the anointing of the sick.

The early Church practiced this sacrament, specifically associating it with the priesthood. Ambrose wrote in the 300s about confession and the power God gives to priests to forgive (or not forgive) sins in His name: "Consider, too, the point that he who has received the Holy Ghost has also received the power of forgiving and of retaining sin. For thus it is written: Receive the Holy Spirit: whosoever sins you forgive, they are forgiven unto them, and whosoever sins you retain, they are retained....The office of the priest is a gift of the Holy Spirit, and His right it is specially to forgive and to retain sins."[13] Hippolytus, Tertullian, Origen, and many other early Christians confirmed sacramental confession to a priest.

It should be obvious by this point that a pattern is developing with regard to this and the other sacraments. They are firmly rooted in the sacred Scriptures, and they were taught and practiced by the Church even in the early centuries.

At first, Luther actually retained the sacrament of confession, along with the Eucharist and baptism, but later he decided that along with all of the sacraments and practices associated with ordained clergy, it had to go. Given his rejection of holy orders, it is not surprising that he would have also rejected this sacrament, which depends upon validly ordained priests and bishops. The other Reformers and all of Protestantism followed his lead, as they had done on so many other fundamental doctrines.

This sacrament, above all others perhaps, incenses Protestant Christians, for the simple reason that they believe that the Bible teaches that only God forgives sin, which must mean that going to a mere human being to receive forgiveness is unbiblical. The verses cited from John 20 are weakly explained away, interpreted as somehow applying to all Christians, or (more often) simply ignored. The witness of the early Christians and Church Fathers on the topic are also ignored.

Catholics agree that it is only God who forgives sin, but since God gives divine authority to man, it is actually God's will that we confess our sins to His priests and receive forgiveness from God through His ministers' lips. Again, it is God's *ordinary* means of grace. A Protestant whole-heartedly and humbly confessing his sins as he has been taught to confess (and this teaching of how to confess varies greatly within Protestantism) doesn't miss out on forgiveness (because God often works in extraordinary ways). However, at the very least, he does miss out on the peace that Catholics enjoy as they leave the confessional with the freedom of knowing that they have been forgiven. At the worst, if a Protestant (or a Catholic for that matter) is rejecting the sacrament of confession out of nothing more than stubborn pride and independence, he might be missing out on a lot more; it certainly doesn't bode well for the sincerity of his repentance.

But a Protestant might object, "God doesn't need a priest in order to forgive me!" And I would reply that he was right—but that I wasn't sure that God's need for man was what was really bothering him but rather *his own* need for man. For many Protestants, it's the audacity and personal insult that God would use another fallible human being like themselves to administer the forgiveness and peace that we all so deeply crave.

It should be noted that the Catholic Church encourages all her members to confess their sins privately in their own hearts to God in prayer as soon as they become aware of them. Catholic Christians can and do directly pray to God daily and have a relationship with Him, but this relationship is not just about "me and Jesus." It involves the Body of Christ, the Church, and it honors Jesus's decision to work through people to administer grace.

Holy Orders and Apostolic Succession

The Catholic Church teaches that a validly ordained priest or bishop is necessary for the administration of several of the sacraments: anointing of the sick, the Eucharist, confirmation, confession, and (interestingly) holy orders, which is the subject of this section. Holy orders, or ordination, is the sacrament by which one becomes a deacon, priest, or bishop. We will focus on the latter two offices here, grouping them under the term "clergy." Without ordained clergy, the aforementioned sacraments cannot be celebrated. (In practice, this fact means that Protestant communities do not have a valid Eucharist—the bread and wine do not become Christ's body and blood—or a valid confirmation.)

The Catechism describes the sacrament:

> Holy Orders is the sacrament through which the mission entrusted by Christ to his apostles continues to be exercised in the Church until the end of time: thus it is the sacrament of apostolic ministry. It includes three degrees: episcopate, presbyterate, and diaconate....The *laying on of hands* by the bishop, with the consecratory prayer, constitutes the visible sign of this ordination.[14]

Martin Luther rejected the distinction between clergy and laity under the banner of "the priesthood of all believers," and so he rejected the sacrament of holy orders. In doing so, he also rejected the doctrine that Christ's divine authority is transmitted through Apostolic Succession. To understand this foundational doctrine, a short explanation is in order. The Catholic Church teaches that it takes a validly ordained bishop to ordain another bishop, but how did the ordaining bishop get ordained? Through other validly ordained bishops. This trail goes back to the Apostles themselves, who were ordained by Jesus Christ. Christ gave the Apostles His divine authority to lead the Church. This authority was then transmitted to the Apostles' successors, the first bishops (like Timothy, whom Paul ordained). The direct line of authority continues down to the current bishops today of the Catholic and Orthodox Churches.

This belief is the doctrine of Apostolic Succession, and Luther knew that he had to reject it; otherwise he could not justify causing a schism from the Church and establishing another church based on his own authority. He and the other Reformers posited a new idea that authority is given by God to whomever "teaches the gospel truthfully," a doctrine sometimes called apostolicity. This doctrine broke the "monopolistic" hold that the Catholic Church had on divine authority and opened up authority to Luther, Calvin, the Anabaptists, and anyone else who thought that they were teaching the truth from the Bible.

Which idea is right: Apostolic Succession or apostolicity? Let's consider a few passages from early Christians, beginning with one from Augustine, the great Church father respected by Catholics and the Protestant Reformers:

> For if the lineal succession of bishops is to be taken into account, with how much more certainty and benefit to the Church do we reckon back till we reach Peter himself, to whom, as bearing in a figure the whole Church, the Lord said: "Upon this rock will I build my Church, and the gates of hell shall not prevail against it!" The successor of Peter was Linus, and his successors in unbroken continuity were these: Clement, Anacletus, Evaristus,

> Alexander, Sixtus...Damasus, and Siricius, whose succes-
> sor is the present Bishop Anastasius.[15]

Clement, the close successor to Peter himself, wrote within the first century:

> The apostles have preached the gospel to us from the
> Lord Jesus Christ; Jesus Christ [has done so] from God.
> Christ therefore was sent forth by God, and the apostles
> by Christ. Both these appointments, then, were made in
> an orderly way, according to the will of God....And thus
> preaching through countries and cities, they appointed
> the first fruits [of their labors], having first proved them
> by the Spirit, to be bishops and deacons of those who
> should afterwards believe. Nor was this any new thing,
> since indeed many ages before it was written concerning
> bishops and deacons. For thus says the Scripture in a cer-
> tain place, "I will appoint their bishops in righteousness,
> and their deacons in faith" Our apostles also knew,
> through our Lord Jesus Christ, that there would be strife
> on account of the office of the episcopate. For this rea-
> son, therefore, inasmuch as they had obtained a perfect
> fore-knowledge of this, they appointed those [ministers]
> already mentioned, and afterwards gave instructions, that
> when these should fall asleep, other approved men
> should succeed them in their ministry.[16]

These excerpts represent only a few of the many writings of the early Christians attesting to Apostolic Succession and the ministerial priesthood. Protestants, however, do not have valid succession from the Apostles, nor do they believe that it is necessary, so they must reject holy orders as the sacrament by which divine authority is transmitted to men by Christ through other ordained men. The Protestant notion of apostolicity—that a man can claim that he teaches God's truth and therefore wields spiritual authority—was a foreign concept to the Church prior to the Reformation.

Joseph Cardinal Ratzinger, now Pope Benedict XVI, explained the sacrament thusly:

> This is precisely what we mean when we call ordination
> of priests a sacrament: ordination is not about the devel-
> opment of one's own powers and gifts. It is not the ap-
> pointment of a man as a functionary because he is espe-
> cially good at it, or because it suits him…it is not a ques-
> tion of a job in which someone secures his own livelih-
> ood by his own abilities, perhaps in order to rise later to
> something better. Sacrament means: I give what I myself
> cannot give; I do something that is not my work; I am on
> a mission and have become the bearer of that which
> another has committed to my charge. Consequently, it is
> also impossible for anyone to declare himself a priest or
> for a community to make someone a priest by its own
> *fiat*. One can receive what is God's only from the sacra-
> ment, by entering into the mission that makes me the
> messenger and instrument of another.[17]

Contrary to this sacramental understanding of the priesthood,
Protestant communities view their ministers, who are "ordained" by
the *fiat* of the community and not through the sacrament, as func-
tionaries rather than as persons specially configured to Christ
through holy orders: both of these Protestant conceptions are
flawed and represent a fundamental misunderstanding of the way
that God instituted rightful authority in His Church.

If Protestantism is true, then the early Church fell into serious error
when she universally proclaimed the doctrine of baptismal regeneration, the real presence of Christ in the Eucharist, the validity of reconciliation, and the other sacraments of the Church. The bishops
of Christ's Church then compounded this error by including elements such as "one baptism for the forgiveness of sins" in the Nicene Creed, the most fundamental formula defining the essentials
of orthodox Christianity.

Contrary to what the disciples of the Apostles and the Church
Fathers taught, Jesus in John 3 must not have been speaking of
baptism when he said that one must "be born of water and the Spirit" but of something else entirely. Likewise, Jesus must not have
been speaking of body and blood when he said, "this is my body"
and "this is my blood" in Matthew 26. And he must have been

speaking metaphorically when he said that His Apostles had the authority to forgive and retain sins in John 20.

And consider confession. In spite of the biblical support and the historical evidence of the early Church's teaching and practice, the sacrament of confession was an evil perversion only done away with in the sixteenth century when the Protestant Reformers rejected it. Christians for 1,500 years lived under the delusion that when they went to the Church and confessed their sins to a priest or bishop, they were truly forgiven by God, when in reality they were placing their trust in a false, human tradition and in their own efforts to run fast enough on the "sacramental treadmill." How many millions of God's precious souls were placed in jeopardy of eternal salvation by this practice?

The Church has demonstrated, then, that her beliefs were corrupted from the very beginning and cannot be trusted to teach the truth on any matter of faith and morals. If she could not preserve the truths taught by the Apostles for even one generation and could not correctly interpret our Lord's words on the sacraments, then she cannot be trusted in her other teachings, either.

Most practically, *if Protestantism is true*, then Protestants have some mighty decisions to make—all on their own, as there is no other true authority than their own interpretation of the Bible. They must decide which Protestant (Luther or Calvin) was right about baptism, which Protestant (Luther or Zwingli) was right about the Eucharist, which Protestants (the liberals or the conservatives) are right about marriage, which of their many and varied teachings on confession and forgiveness are valid, etc. I don't envy the Protestants this task.

Chapter Nine
Tradition

Few words misinform Catholic-Protestant relations more than tradition. Especially for Evangelical Protestants, it nearly always refers to man-made, arbitrary practices that seem to run counter to the truth of God. The passages where Christ upbraids the scribes and Pharisees for their hypocrisy and man-made traditions are often quoted as proof that tradition in the spiritual sense is intrinsically bad. Other Protestants who trace their origins deeper in history and understand better the magisterial Reformers, believe that some traditions can be good and that *sola Scriptura* does not mean that all ideas outside of the Bible are to be shunned. Luther, Zwingli, and Calvin all looked to the early Church Fathers and to the practice of the Faith in the early centuries of the Church for insights and wisdom into how to accurately interpret the Scriptures. For both Protestant positions, however, no tradition should be accepted that contradicts a truth from Scripture, and no tradition whatsoever is *binding* upon a Christian, for everything essential and binding for Christians to believe and live by is found in Scripture. Other ideas may be useful but they are not in themselves necessary for salvation.

For Catholics, tradition is something far more important. Firstly, there are traditions (with a lower-case t), which are customs or practices within the Church that can and do change. And then there is sacred Tradition, which contains the deposit of Faith given by Christ to the Church through the Apostles. This sacred Tradition has two parts: the written portion is sacred Scripture and the unwritten portion is (a bit confusingly) also referred to simply as "Tradition." So when a Catholic uses the word "Tradition," he is usually referring to the unwritten part of the deposit of Faith (though much has been written in explanation of Tradition—most notably in the Catechism of the Catholic Church).

Sacred Tradition is not just a static set of information or data that the Church has preserved in a box under the Vatican; it is instead a living thing. Pope Benedict explains: "We have seen that it [Tradition] is not a collection of things or words, like a box of dead things. Tradition is the river of new life that proceeds from the origins, from Christ to us, and makes us participate in God's history with humanity."[1] This living Tradition is the river that flows from Christ, Who is its spring, and makes Him ever present to His Church and thus to us, her members. It is dynamic and alive, given to us by the Holy Spirit in the sacramental life of the Church. It is one primary way that our Lord is with us, even to the end of the age.

Many Protestant ears prick up when hearing that there is some mysterious "unwritten" truth that Tradition communicates to us. What exactly are these unwritten truths? How do we know that they are true? To understand Tradition, we must first realize that Christ taught His Apostles many things that were not written down, as John mentions at the end of his gospel: "There are also many other things that Jesus did, but if these were to be described individually, I do not think the whole world would contain the books that would be written" (John 21:25). Earlier in John, Jesus says, "I have much more to tell you, but you cannot bear it now. But when he comes, the Spirit of truth, he will guide you to all truth" (John 16:12–13). What were these things that Jesus taught His Apostles? Protestantism does not have an answer for that question and must assert that whatever else Jesus taught them, it was not important enough to be included in the Scriptures, which are the sole repository for the important truths of the Faith. The Catholic Church, however, declares that this divine wisdom was not lost but was given to the Apostles as the authorized leaders of the Church and preserved in the living Tradition through their successors by the Holy Spirit's power and guidance.

We will look at a few examples of Tradition in this chapter, but one that we have already examined is the doctrine of the perpetual virginity of Mary. This doctrine has been believed by Christians since the beginning of the Church's existence, yet the Bible nowhere declares it to be true. Instead, a superficial reading of the Scriptures would indicate that Mary and Joseph had marital relations just like any other married couple and subsequently had several more children. Yet, as we discussed in an earlier section, Luther and Zwingli affirmed this doctrine as true and Calvin was favorable toward it, for they did not eschew all of the Catholic Church's Tradition. They knew that this doctrine was taught from time immemorial and was completely consistent with the Bible, if interpreted properly. Only the Radical Reformers (the Anabaptists) rejected this doctrine, because it was not found explicitly in the Bible. The perpetual virginity of Mary is a doctrine firmly held in sacred Tradition, one that is in harmony with the Scriptures but not explicit in them.

The Closure of Public Revelation

All Christians believe that *public revelation* by God to man ended with the death of the last Apostle. The Catholic Encyclopedia describes public revelation:

> It remains here to distinguish the Christian [public] Revelation or "deposit of faith" from what are termed private revelations. This distinction is of importance: for while the Church recognizes that God has spoken to His servants in every age, and still continues thus to favour chosen souls, she is careful to distinguish these revelations from the Revelation which has been committed to her charge, and which she proposes to all her members for their acceptance. That Revelation was given in its entirety to Our Lord and His apostles. After the death of the last of the twelve it could receive no increment.[2]

What is interesting about this truth is that Protestants accept it, too, even though no passage in the Bible states that public revelation will end at the death of the last Apostle. The important Protestant document called the Westminster Confession of Faith declares:

> The whole counsel of God concerning all things necessary for His own glory, man's salvation, faith and life, is either expressly set down in Scripture, or by good and necessary consequence may be deduced from Scripture: unto which nothing at any time is to be added, whether by new revelations of the Spirit, or traditions of men.[3]

We see here that a Reformed Protestant confession asserts this doctrine of public revelation's closure to be true but does so without any basis in the Scriptures! No biblical verses support this declaration.

Where then did this teaching, held universally by all Christian traditions, come from? The answer is sacred Tradition, and yet no Protestant voices an objection against this (extra-biblical) teaching. It is actually a necessary underpinning of *sola Scriptura*, because if the Scriptures can be added to over time through additional public revelation, then the Scriptures are a changing foundation.[4]

This doctrine of closed revelation, like the contents of the canon itself, is a binding truth that *must* be accepted by all the Protestant faithful, yet it does not appear in the Scriptures anywhere. The Catholic Church teaches about Tradition that "this truth and teaching are contained in written books and in the unwritten traditions that the apostles received from Christ himself or that were handed on, as it were from hand to hand, from the apostles under the inspiration of the Holy Spirit, and so have come down to us."[5]

Protestants frequently attack *other* truths found in the unwritten part of Tradition (like the Virgin Mary's Immaculate Conception), even ridiculing the idea by asserting that these unwritten traditions were handed on from one person to the next as in the game of Telephone, where the original message gets garbled as it passes along the chain of people, until what comes out from the last person to hear it bears no resemblance to the original. But they don't make the same argument against public revelation being ended, because they believe it with all their hearts (and have to believe it to hold to *sola Scriptura*).

If Protestantism is true, then public revelation is closed. However, it is *also* true that this fact has no direct biblical support, which creates a contradiction.

Oral Tradition and John's Third Letter

John the Evangelist lived during the time of Gnosticism's rise under Simon the Magician in the first century and its promulgation by a man named Cerinthus in the second. John opposed Cerinthus with vigor:

There are also those who heard from him that John, the
disciple of the Lord, going to bathe at Ephesus, and per-
ceiving Cerinthus within, rushed out of the bath-house
without bathing, exclaiming, "Let us fly, lest even the
bath-house fall down, because Cerinthus, the enemy of
the truth, is within."[6]

The Gnostics claimed to have *secret knowledge* that was necessary
for salvation. The Apostles and their successors opposed the Gnostics at every turn, proclaiming that God's truth had been entrusted
to the Church and was available to everyone who sought it, not just
an elite few.

John, the last living Apostle, still drew breath, and yet already
there were those who were opposing him, his authority, and the
truth of Christ. In 3 John, we read this fascinating passage:

I have written something to the church, but Diotrephes,
who likes to put himself first, does not acknowledge my
authority. So if I come, I will bring up what he is doing,
prating against me with evil words....I had much to write
to you, but I would rather not write with pen and ink; I
hope to see you soon, and we will talk together face to
face (3 John 9–10,13–14).

It is clear that John believes he has *authority* and expects the
churches to submit to his authority. Diotrephes is not doing so but
is instead actively opposing John, arrogating authority to himself
that he does not have, against the Apostle of Christ. The next verse
is also remarkable as it is one of the verses where an Apostle in-
forms the churches that he would prefer to talk personally with
them (others throughout the New Testament include Phil. 1:26 and
Rom. 1:8–15).

What *did* John tell the church when he later visited and spoke to
them? We don't have it written down. If *sola Scriptura* were true, it
would be quite strange for John to tell one of his churches that he
had much to tell them but preferred to visit them in person instead
of writing it down. He acts as if the important thing is his living,
personal witness to Christ and that he has full confidence that these
orally delivered truths will be preserved in the Church without nec-

essarily being written down in the canonical Scriptures. Hence we have his third letter, an incredibly short missive, which gives only the briefest of glimpses into the life of the Church in the late first century and tells us nothing of what he actually said when he visited the church.

The Catholic Church explains that these truths have been secured in the living river that is the Tradition of Christ's Church, which gives us God's full revelation to man, safeguarded by the Holy Spirit and made available to us today in the Church's teachings and sacramental life. Since God willed that people should know these truths revealed in and by Christ, He also willed that all Christians afterwards should have access to them so that they could live in the truth and be set free by it. These truths are contained both in the sacred Scriptures and in the living Tradition of the Church.

If Protestantism is true, then *sola Scriptura* is true. So passages where oral tradition is commended are to be disregarded, and times where we know the Apostles spoke to the churches things not recorded in the Scriptures must be written off as unknowable. Further, Christianity has essentially lost all of the wisdom and God-given truth that was not written down in the (relatively short) New Testament books.

Evangelical Protestantism and Tradition

One of my Anglican friends wanted to buy a book by Augustine, one of the giants of the Christian faith who is known as the "Doctor of Grace." He happened to be close to a popular Evangelical Christian bookstore, so he stopped in and looked around. Not finding the book, he approached the person working at the store to ask where he could find it: "Pardon me, where are your books by Augustine?" The employee looked at him blankly and responded, "Augustine *who?*" Apparently this store—part of a prolific Evangelical chain—doesn't carry even a single book by Augustine.

Now this is a funny situation, and I laughed when my friend related it to me, but I do not intend to insult Christians who don't know who Augustine is, especially since I myself was baptized in an Evangelical Protestant church. However, it does demonstrate an endemic problem with Evangelical Protestant Christianity: they have largely forgotten men and women who came before them in the Christian faith, those giants on whose shoulders (and prayers) they now stand. Christianity didn't end in the year 100 when the Bible was finished being written and then resume again 1,500 years later when the first Baptists founded a new ecclesial community. But going into this Christian store, one is hard pressed to find a book written in the time period between the Bible and the twentieth century.

Instead of standing on the shoulders of Christian giants, many Protestants seek to discover all truth themselves with their Bible and the Spirit. This desire to reinvent the Christian wheel is especially prevalent in Evangelicalism, stemming perhaps from the influence of the Radical Reformers, who were not impressed by Luther, Zwingli, and Calvin and instead took the magisterial Reformers' ideas to their logical end: the individual can interpret Scripture and needs not rely on any human opinion (except their own, of course). As a result, most Evangelicals know little about the magisterial Reformers and care even less about them.

One of the events that led to this antitraditional bent of Evangelicals was the revivalism of the First and Second Great Awakenings in the United States 200 years ago. Mark Noll, an Evangelical Protestant historian, vividly described this phenomenon:

> The problem with revivalism for the life of the mind, however, lay precisely in its antitraditionalism. Revivals called people to Christ as a way of escaping tradition, including traditional learning. They called upon individuals to take the step of faith for themselves. In so doing, they often led to the impression that individual believers could accept nothing from others. Everything of value in the Christian life had to come from the individual's own choice—not just personal faith but every scrap of wisdom, understanding, and conviction about the faith. This dismissal of tradition was no better illustrated than in a memorable comment by two Kentucky revivalists early in the nineteenth century. When quotations from [John] Calvin were used to argue against Robert Marshall and J. Thompson, they replied, "We are not personally acquainted with the writings of John Calvin, nor are we

certain how nearly we agree with his views of divine
truths; neither do we care."[7]

Even though Evangelicals owe many of their most important beliefs to John Calvin's influence, through the revival spirit of antitra-
ditionalism, many denied any connection with him and did not even
have a basic understanding of who he was. Fast forward to today,
and the situation is much the same. In my conversations with an
Evangelical friend of mine, he said almost the same thing to me: "I
don't care what Luther or any other Protestant teaches," much less
what some Christian from the second century said—even if he was
a disciple of John the Evangelist, the beloved Apostle of Jesus! Why
don't he and other Evangelicals care what Luther or anyone else
says? Because my friend has the Holy Spirit dwelling within him,
and he has his Bible, so he believes from those he can individually
come to know divine truth.

Lest we think that it is only "Protestants in the pews" who are
confused or ignorant of history and tradition, consider Evangelical
author William Webster, who wrote a book called *The Church of
Rome at the Bar of History*, which seeks to discredit the Catholic
Church. In his section on Thomas Aquinas, the incredibly faithful
and intellectually gifted Catholic saint and Doctor of the Church,
Webster "summarizes" Aquinas's teachings in the *Summa Theologiae*
in a grand total of six sentences, claiming that Aquinas taught that
faith in the Church is vital to salvation but faith in Jesus Christ was
not. This is an utterly false claim.[8]

Webster's treatise is a grave disservice to Christians who read his
book. To dismiss Aquinas in such a capricious way is irresponsible
at best. It would be equivalent to a scientist of our day dismissing
Einstein, Newton, Galileo, and Copernicus by first mischaracteriz-
ing all of their discoveries and then (falsely) concluding that they
were poor scientists. Thomas Aquinas believed in Jesus Christ with
all his heart, mind, and strength and devoted his life to understanding and promulgating the truth of Christ. This astounding treatment
of Aquinas by Mr. Webster is indicative of the shallow and often
skewed understanding of Christian history and tradition by some
Protestants, even Protestant apologists.

If (Evangelical) Protestantism is true, then it is possible (and preferable) for Christians in each new generation to figure out all truth for themselves, with nothing but the Bible as a guide.

The Family of God Versus "Me and God"

The Catholic Church teaches a doctrine called the *communion of saints*, which the Catholic Encyclopedia calls the

> spiritual solidarity which binds together the faithful on earth, the souls in purgatory, and the saints in heaven in the organic unity of the same mystical body under Christ its head....The participants in that solidarity are called saints by reason of their destination [heaven] and of their partaking of the fruits of the Redemption.[9]

This ancient belief has its roots in the Bible's references to the Church being "the household of God" (see Eph. 2:19), whose members are the Christian faithful. Since we know that those who die in Christ do not die eternally but rather still live in Christ awaiting the Resurrection, the faithful who have died in God's friendship remain united to the Church, which is Christ's Body (see Eph. 4:4–13). The Church as a supernatural society extends beyond the currently living. Based on these truths, since we Christians pray for one another here on earth, we also receive graces from the prayers of the saints in Heaven and can pray for the saints being purified in purgatory. Though we cannot see them, we know that they are with God and are members of His Church, as we are.

Protestants reject the teaching that we can pray for those who have fallen asleep in Christ, and they reject purgatory as well. These Catholic teachings were some of the first ones that Martin Luther denounced, leading all other Protestants to follow his example. Their rejection of these doctrines comes from the alleged fact that they are not found explicitly in the Bible. Other reasons given are that those who have died in Christ are dead and therefore completely disconnected from us and that the existence of purgatory implies that Jesus's death for our sins was insufficient.

To the objection that those who have died in Christ are dead and therefore no communion with them is possible, the account of the Transfiguration poses a solid rebuttal. The great Old Testament men, Moses and Elijah, appear before Jesus—and Peter, James, and John: "And behold, Moses and Elijah appeared to them, conversing with him" (Matt. 17:1–8). Peter even wanted to pitch a tent for each of them! Couple this account of two "dead" men talking with Jesus with the revelation that Jesus used to refute the Sadducees in their denial of the Resurrection: "That the dead will rise even Moses made known in the passage about the bush, when he called 'Lord' the God of Abraham, the God of Isaac, and the God of Jacob; and he is not God of the dead, but of the living, for to him all are alive" (Luke 20:37–38). We see that those who have died on earth are still very much alive to God and even able to communicate with those on earth because God desires it and makes it possible.

The objection that purgatory implies a deficiency in Jesus's death for us is based on the common but erroneous misunderstanding of Catholic teachings. In Protestantism, there is only one kind of sin rather than a distinct difference between venial and mortal sins. So since Protestants think that all sin is of the same degree, and Jesus forgives sins, the Protestant reasons that a Catholic believes Jesus has only forgiven a portion of sins but the rest inspire punishment. The Catholic teaching, on the other hand, groups lesser sins as *venial* and serious ones done deliberately with a full understanding of their evil as *mortal*. A person who commits a mortal sin and does not repent before she dies cannot be forgiven in purgatory; rather, the sad soul in such a state at her death goes to Hell, as she has chosen to reject God by committing such evil.

Purgatory is for the Christian who dies with venial sins on his soul and who has some degree of attachment to things sinful; such a person is in a state of sanctifying grace, because he loves God and has not driven God out of his soul through mortal sin. The Christians in purgatory benefit from our prayers, because God speeds their purification so that they enter Heaven all the more quickly. Of course, purgatory, like Heaven, is outside of time, so the allusions to periods of time and speed are only analogies used to help us grasp the concepts.

If Protestantism is true, then the individualism of modern Evangelical Christianity here on earth extends to those who have fallen asleep in Christ as well. We have no connection to those brethren who have gone to their reward in Christ, for God keeps us all separate from one another, in spite of the Church being called His family. The witness of the early Christians, of the Church, and of the Bible[10] to praying for the souls of those who have died are all a deception.

Chapter Ten
The Scriptures

Bryce is a Presbyterian friend of mine with a razor-sharp intellect. He had found great success at work and was happily married, with two children. His church was spinning off a new community, and so greatly respected were his abilities that he was asked to be one of the new church's elders. (The elders in Protestant churches are responsible for important decisions concerning the community, and in Presbyterian churches, the group of elders is called "the session.")

He was friends with the pastor of the new church, and they had many good conversations about their faith. But when the pastor moved away, the problems began. Without a pastor, it became up to the session to run the church and decide doctrinal issues. Bryce didn't know how to respond to certain hot-button topics that were now open for discussion. People in the congregation and in the session were interpreting the Bible in contradictory ways. "How do I know which interpretation is correct?" he wondered. He felt frustrated and overwhelmed; finally, he began to consider changing churches.

Bryce also noticed that many churches he visited were centered around the charisma and person of their pastor, almost to the point where Jesus was obscured. This troubled him deeply. He also became disillusioned by the substantial differences between congregations that supposedly belonged to the same "flavor" of Presbyterianism. One congregation had abolished male-centered language for God and had moved to inclusive, gender-neutral language. They liked to talk about the "Kindom of God," rather than the "Kingdom," (which they said had patriarchal connotations).

He and his wife eventually found a new Presbyterian church. But their time there was short-lived. He watched the new church stumble through the search procedure to find an associate pastor. Instead of witnessing the Holy Spirit at work in this process, he saw petty politics and political correctness. The final straw came when, as he took his family up to communion, the new associate pastor asked if his son "would like a piece of bread." He knew in his heart that communion meant so much more.

All of these inconsistencies and problems led Bryce to a crucial decision. Either God existed and He provided a way for us to know Him and the truth, or He simply didn't exist. A man dedicated to principles and truth, he was suspicious of people who said that their church "felt right," or was a "good fit" for them. To him, the Catholic way wasn't easy, but he saw that fact as a hallmark of its truth.

Eventually he started talking with a Catholic friend of his, who met him at an intellectual level and didn't actively try to get him to convert. Also, one of the priests in the local diocese—who is now a good friend of his—was happy to meet one-on-one on many occasions to answer his questions. The conversations with these faithful Catholics, coupled with God's grace, resulted in his eventual conversion and completion of RCIA. Today, Bryce offers this advice to people with questions about the Catholic Church: "Stop speculating, and just go talk to a priest and get answers straight from the Church itself!"

Are the Scriptures Difficult to Understand?

Let us consider two passages from 1 John: "If we say, 'We are without sin,' we deceive ourselves, and the truth is not in us" (1 John 1:8) and "No one who remains in him [Jesus] sins; no one who sins has seen him or known him" (1 John 3:6).

An apparent contradiction exists here: from the first passage, it is clear that if we claim we do not sin, we are liars, because we do sin. But the most straightforward interpretation of the second passage is that if we remain in Jesus, we do not sin. Since we believe the Scriptures to be inerrant, this contradiction must only be an *apparent* one, so how can these two verses be reconciled?

Most Protestant Christians who read this passage decide that in the second passage, John must mean "persists in sinning" or "sins and doesn't repent." Otherwise it would mean that if we commit a sin, which most of us do fairly often, we do not know Jesus—sounds pretty harsh and unreasonable. Catholics, however, draw a distinction between two degrees of sin: mortal and venial. Mortal sin is so grave that the Christian loses the divine life of God in his soul and thus falls from a state of sanctifying grace, putting him in peril of eternal damnation. Venial sin is of a lesser degree and does not cause the Christian to lose sanctifying grace. With this distinction, it is possible to understand John's words as meaning that no Christian who remains in Jesus continues to sin *mortally*, because to do so is to reject God in a drastic way, refusing to abide in Christ. Depending upon one's interpretive tradition, whether Catholic or some strain of Protestant, either interpretation could resolve this apparent contradiction. So which one is true?

Let us consider another passage in 1 John: "As for you, the anointing that you received from him remains in you, *so that you do not need anyone to teach you*. But his anointing teaches you about everything and is true and not false; just as it taught you, remain in him" (1 John 2:27, emphasis mine).

The simplest interpretation of this passage would be that we Christians do not need anyone to teach us, because we received the anointing from Christ, the Holy Spirit. He will teach us all we need to know. A logical deduction from this passage combined with the ones that tell us we are all priests is that we do not need a ministerial priesthood or perhaps any type of pastor at all.

Some Protestants do indeed point to this passage as defense against needing *any* human authorities or teachers, claiming that the Holy Spirit teaches them directly. Most do not go to that extreme and are willing to accept human authorities, at least so long as they are properly elected or display an agreeable level of spiritual knowledge. But they will still use this passage to claim for themselves a sort of "sanctified intuition," whereby their own thoughts or ideas are all of the Holy Spirit and perhaps superior to their leaders'. Catholics see this verse as needing to be understood in the context of the Church, of which John was a prominent leader. The Church of Christ is the only teacher they need—they do not need to be taught by the wicked men referenced in the previous verses, which is what John was possibly alluding to in saying they do not need teachers.

The point is that the Scriptures are not so obviously clear that we can all read them and come to the same conclusions. Even 1 John, which is a short book, contains many passages where the most obvious interpretation is not always the correct one.

A Protestant might object that the key to interpreting these verses is to "use Scripture to interpret Scripture," such that unclear or seemingly contradictory verses will be made clear or resolved by looking to other verses.

There is a certain degree of truth in this claim; however, using it as a rule to understand the Scriptures just pushes the question of interpretation back to those other verses and is also complicated by the fact that there are many verses from which to choose to help explain the problematic one. With the New Testament alone containing thousands of verses, how do we know which ones to choose? And what if we interpret those other verses wrongly in the first place? Then we are left in the sad state of using a false interpretation to explain another verse, which can only lead to further error.

For example, a Catholic would point to the end of John 6 as a key to helping us know what Jesus meant when, at the Last Supper, he said, "Take and eat; this is my body" (Matt. 26:26). Using John 6 (as interpreted by many saints and fathers of the early Church), Jesus must have meant that the bread and wine truly became His flesh and blood. A Protestant, however, would reject that interpretation of John 6 *and also* deny any connection between it and the Last Supper. Instead, a Protestant would point to all of the places where Jesus speaks figuratively of Himself as being the key to understanding His symbolism when saying, "this is my body." Which interpretation is right, and which set of verses should be looked to as primary keys in helping us to understand the other verses?

If Protestantism is true, then the Scriptures can be understood through careful study and correct examination of "the Scriptures as a whole" as well as through other particular verses that are ostensibly clearer. When faithful members of Protestant communities diligently and prayerfully seek to understand the Scriptures and yet arrive at radically different interpretations of the Bible on important matters of faith and morals, at least one must have erred due to sloppy scholarship, erroneous interpretive paradigms, or lack of faithful attentiveness to the Holy Spirit. These truth seekers must then decide if the error now calls for denominational action—a new split.

Protestantism's Lack of Interpretive Authority

At the root of the endemic contradictions within Protestantism lies the absence (and by definition, the impossibility) of an *interpretive authority* for the Scriptures above that of the individual Christian. Protestants cannot accept that any person or group has this authority, because Protestantism holds the *Bible itself* to be the ultimate authority. Ideally, the interpretation of the Bible would be in harmony among Protestants, but this has never been so for the group's entire history.

It is thus a valid question to ask a Protestant: How do you know that your interpretation of the Bible is correct against the interpretation of every other Protestant? The short answer is, he doesn't know for sure. And he would probably consider it dangerously cult-like to claim otherwise. But if the Holy Spirit is guiding this man, how could he be steered wrong?

Recall that Martin Luther and Ulrich Zwingli taught conflicting interpretations of the Bible with regard to the Lord's Supper and how, exactly, Christ was "present" in the Eucharist. Luther believed that Christ was indeed present in the Eucharist while Zwingli thought His presence to be purely figurative.

Alister McGrath analyzes this situation and the problem is poses for Protantism:

> It will be obvious that these represent totally different readings of the same text. Luther's interpretation was much more traditional, Zwingli's more radical. Which was right? And which was Protestant? We see here the fundamental difficulty that the Reformation faced: the absence of any authoritative interpreter of scripture that could give rulings on contested matters of biblical interpretation. The question was not simply whether Luther or Zwingli was right: it was whether the emerging Protestant movement possessed the means to resolve such questions of biblical interpretation. If the Bible had ultimate authority, who had the right to interpret the Bible? This was no idle question, and it lay at the heart of Protestantism's complex relationship with its core text. For this question to be answered, an authoritative rule or

principle had to be proposed that stood *above* scripture—
the very idea of which was ultimately anathema to Protestantism. The three leading Reformers—Luther, Zwingli, and Calvin—all recognized the importance of the
question; significantly, each offered a different answer.[1]

We see from McGrath's history of the Reformation that, due to
the disjointed reform movements independently springing up in
different countries in the 1520s, Protestantism's very foundation
was one of disunity, lacking an authority that could decide whose
biblical interpretation was the correct one. Keith Mathison, a Reformed Protestant author who penned an influential book titled *The
Shape of Sola Scriptura*, also wrote about this important issue:

> All appeals to Scripture are appeals to interpretations of
> Scripture. The only real question is: whose interpreta-
> tion? People with differing interpretations of Scripture
> cannot set a Bible on a table and ask it to resolve their
> differences. In order for the Scripture to function as an
> authority, it must be read and interpreted by someone.[2]

Who is that "someone" who reads and interprets the Bible with
authority in Protestantism? The fact that Protestants (like Catholics)
claim the Bible to be inerrant does not help them out of this bind,
either. McGrath trenchantly explains this dilemma:

> It is perfectly possible for an inerrant text to be inter-
> preted incorrectly. Asserting the infallibility of a text
> merely accentuates the importance of the interpreter of
> that text. Unless the interpreter is also thought of as in-
> fallible—a view that Protestantism has rejected, associat-
> ing it with the Catholic views of the church or papacy—
> the issue of determining the "right" meaning of the Bible
> is not settled, or even addressed, by declaring that the sa-
> cred text is infallible.[3]

A Catholic can certainly agree that, regardless of whether an infallible interpreter exists, having an inerrant book is better than having an error-filled book, but that fact does not mean that having an

infallible interpreter is not objectively better than having a fallible one.

If Protestantism is true, then there is no infallible interpreter of the Scriptures and thus no interpreter can be accepted as authoritative. God did inspire the Scriptures to be without error, but He did not provide an authoritative, infallible *interpreter* for the inerrant Scriptures, leaving us with only conflicting, error-prone opinions of people. The Scriptures must therefore be deemed to be sufficiently clear for most people on all *important* matters of the faith. Since, even between the founders of Protestantism, no accord could be reached on what Jesus meant at the Last Supper, then the proper meaning of "body" and "blood" must simply not be significant, and the Reformers were quibbling over trifles.

The Perspicuity of the Scriptures

Are the Scriptures clear (perspicuous)? That is, can a literate, faithful Christian read the Bible and understand what God is saying? The answer depends upon how high or low we set the bar for "understanding" and how much or how little we allow for differences in that understanding. For example, setting the bar low, all Christians would agree that the Bible teaches that Jesus Christ came for our salvation by dying on the Cross. Further, the belief that Jesus was both truly God and truly man is a teaching that *most* Christians throughout history have held, though both of those doctrines were challenged in significant ways in early Christian history. But once we go a bit more in-depth and get into such questions as *how* Jesus saves a person and *what*, exactly, one needs to do in order to be saved by Christ, we run into all manner of differences among Christian traditions.

Protestantism teaches that the Scriptures are clear—despite any person's experience to the contrary. Consider the words of Martin Luther:

> All the *things*, therefore, contained in the Scriptures, are made manifest, although some *places*, from the words not being understood, are yet obscure....And, if the words are obscure in one place, yet they are clear in another....But,

> if many things still remain abstruse to many, this does
> not arise from obscurity in the Scriptures, but from their
> own blindness or want of understanding, who do not go
> the way to see the all-perfect clearness of the truth.[4]

Luther claimed here that the Scriptures are very clear and that those who find them otherwise have only themselves to blame.

But biblical verses exist that actually refute the perspicuity of the Scriptures. Here is one from Peter's second epistle: "So also our beloved brother Paul wrote to you according to the wisdom given him, speaking of this as he does in all his letters. There are some things in them hard to understand, which the ignorant and unstable twist to their own destruction, as they do the other scriptures" (2 Pet. 3:15–16). The fact that the inspired Scriptures say that the inspired Scriptures can be "hard to understand" cannot be easily dismissed. Peter's statement assumes that there are stable, wise persons leading the Church who understand the Scriptures rightly and do *not* twist them to pervert the truth. However, even with this ability to rightly understand the Scriptures, Peter says outright that some of Paul's writings are "hard to understand."

And indeed, it is usually a verse or two of Paul's that is referenced in the differences that divide many Protestant communities. The Calvinists' beliefs on predestination and free will quote Paul, as do the Baptists', and both contradict Catholic teaching, which also quotes Paul. The problem is that, depending upon which verses are stressed and used as the interpretive keys for understanding other verses, any one of these ideas about God's omniscience and our human free will could be correct. The Bible can be interpreted to fit mutually exclusive paradigms.

Other contradictory teachings include whether one can "lose" one's salvation or not, how one is justified, the role of works in one's justification and sanctification, how the Holy Spirit speaks to us, and whether miracles and charismatic gifts are still given by God to us today—not to mention rulings on all the moral issues of our time. Given the number of faithful, intelligent persons in these different communities, Luther's argument that these other Christians who believed differently than he did were idiotic or unfaithful simply doesn't hold water. Something else must be true, and the only possibility is that the Scriptures are not clear to the degree that Protestants claim them to be.

Does the Catholic Church say that no one can understand the Bible, so that Christians should not even try to read the Scriptures? By no means! The Bible can be read and understood aright. However, the Catholic Church does give these guidelines for reading and understanding them: firstly, the reader should be especially attentive "to the content and unity of the whole Scripture." Secondly, one should read the Scripture within "the living tradition of the whole Church." And thirdly, the reader should be attentive to the analogy of faith. The first point is accepted by all Protestants: one must read the Scriptures as a whole and not just slice it up piecemeal into isolated parts. The Scriptures form a cohesive whole and must be read as such.

The second point, however, Protestants find problematic. It means that a Christian should read the Bible within the living Tradition of Christ's Church, which subsists in the Catholic Church. Some Protestants could agree that early Christian writers, saints, and Church Fathers should be (very selectively) looked to and taken into account when reading the Scriptures, but no Protestant believes that the Catholic Church's living Tradition is a divinely established entity, much less a trustworthy one. The Catholic Church, however, believing herself to be guided by God "into all truth" as Jesus promised the Apostles (see John 16:13), exhorts Christians to read the Bible in the divinely sheltered valley of the Church's Spirit-guided Tradition to avoid going astray. God designed His Church to be the agent whereby His truth was safeguarded for all humanity, and the inerrant Scriptures were both written and discerned as God-breathed by that same Church. It thus makes total sense that the authoritative interpretation of the Scriptures also belongs to Christ's Church, the Catholic Church, which Christ built in the first century and continues to build on the foundation of His Apostles (see Eph. 2:20). Finally, the "analogy of faith" consists of things like the Nicene Creed, which summarize the essential doctrines of our faith.[5]

If Protestantism is true, then the Scriptures must be so internally clear that a faithful, studious Christian can come to an accurate interpretation of them. (If this claim were not true, then how could the Scriptures be the ultimate authority over all Christians?) When one Christian, then, contradicts another on any important matter, one or both must be either unfaithful (refusing to hear God) or else immature (too ignorant to hear God). God gave us, then, a perfectly clear Bible, but it's apparently up to us to get good enough to interpret it. And Protestantism's sea of conflicting voices, each claiming to interpret the Bible correctly, is strong evidence against the perspicuity of the Scriptures.

Misinterpreting the Great Commission

Protestants are seen today as great missionaries, and rightfully so, as thousands of Protestant Christians live as full-time missionaries in far-off lands, to say nothing of the seasonal or one-time missionaries who seek to spread the gospel every year. Yet during the time of the Reformation and for centuries after, almost no Protestants went on any missions at all!

The "Great Commission" is described in the last verses of Matthew's gospel, when Jesus is about to ascend to Heaven, and He gives the Apostles the command to go out into all the nations to baptize and teach them. Protestants today confidently point to those verses as the biblical motivation for their great missionary journeys throughout the world, arguing that this command was made to the Apostles but of course was intended for all Christians as well. Most Protestants don't realize that this modern-day Protestant interpretation is a fairly recent novelty within their ranks. For the first two to three hundred years after the Reformers, Protestants understood this passage as Jesus telling *the Apostles only* to go and spread the good news and that that work had been accomplished sufficiently by the Apostles and perhaps the few generations after them. Unfortunately, the Bible did not make clear whether Jesus was talking only to the Apostles or whether He intended this command for those that came after them as well.

The Catholic Church, on the other hand, has always understood this passage as being intended for all Christians, and ironically, while the Protestant Reformers were proclaiming their novel interpretation of these verses and going on no missionary journeys, one of the greatest missionaries of all time, Francis Xavier, was leaving the European shores for Asia to bring the gospel to peoples who had never heard it (in Japan, Borneo, and India). The Protestant Reformers and their disciples for centuries after them concentrated their efforts instead at converting existing Catholics to Protestantism, confident in their (erroneous) interpretation of the Great Commission.

If (modern) Protestantism is true, its laudable missionary zeal is still in direct contradiction to the teachings of its founders.

Interpreting the Bible with a Modern, Scientific Mind

One day, I was reading some Scripture, and an error came to mind that we modern Christians often make when interpreting biblical passages. Here are the verses that caught my attention (from Acts 13:22–26): "In those days Paul said: 'God raised up David as king; of him God testified, I have found David, son of Jesse, a man after my own heart; he will carry out my every wish.' " Now, we all know that David lusted after Bathsheba, committed adultery with her, and sent her husband to die on the front lines of his army. So, is God a liar when he says that David is a man after his own heart and that he would carry out God's *every* wish? Or maybe God was simply mistaken about David?

Of course, God always tells the truth and is never tricked, and so it is an error of interpretation if we take these words in their "scientifically literal" sense, where the word "every" has no exception and must mean that David never sinned and always did what God willed. Clearly, God condemned David's sins, and he was punished for them (either directly or through his children). However, David repented and was forgiven. So just as David's evil deeds were certainly not conforming him to God's own heart, all the same, David was a man after the heart of God, asking earnestly and humbly for forgiveness and repenting of his sins.

An oft-quoted passage by Protestants is from Romans 3:23: "all have sinned and are deprived of the glory of God." They highlight the word "all" to allegedly prove that the Virgin Mary sinned during her life. Therefore, they reason, the Catholic doctrines of her Immaculate Conception and sinless life are false. Of course, using the scientifically literal meaning, the word "all" means "everyone without exception." Protestants immediately exclude Jesus from this list (and rightfully so), but they claim that no one else should be excluded, since Jesus is a special case.

The fact is that assuming "all" means "everyone" here is reading a scientifically precise meaning into the word that Paul did not intend. It is possible that another exception exists, and the Virgin Mary could, by a special act of God's grace, be that one. This fact does not by any means prove that she was preserved from sin throughout her life, but it does mean that it is dubious to try to prove with this verse that she did sin.

The previous verses in this same chapter help to demonstrate my principle as well: "There is no one just, not one, there is no one who understands, there is no one who seeks God. All have gone astray; all alike are worthless; there is not one who does good, (there is not) even one" (Rom. 3:10–12). Wow, *no one* seeks God? *All* are worthless? We read previously in the Old Testament that David was a man after God's own heart, fulfilling his every wish, and throughout the Bible are many examples of men and women who faithfully followed our Lord. So clearly these verses must not be taken as meaning that every person is "worthless" in a universal sense (we know God values every person infinitely) or that no person has ever existed who sought God.

If Protestantism is true, then we should be able to read the Bible and correctly interpret it, but as this section has shown, it is easy to misunderstand many passages of the Bible when we read them through our modern interpretive lens.

Conclusion
To Find the Truth, Follow the Trail of Authority

For every argument that has been made in this book, a Protestant apologist could attempt a response, perhaps more eloquent and well-presented than mine. The very existence of this debate, continuing now for almost five centuries, underscores the need for each Christian to methodically explore the arguments and listen to the responses from both Protestants and Catholics in order to discern, with God's help and with much prayer and humility, where the fullness of the truth resides. This book makes the claim, particularly against Protestantism, that the fullness of the truth is found in the Catholic Church. It has explored scores of individual issues, each section highlighting the *central* issue of authority, from a different vantage point.

Lack of any centralized authority has proven to be Protestantism's Achilles's heel, and the arguments of this book strike at it. Every difference between Catholics and Protestants ultimately stems from their beliefs about the source of God-given human authority in this world. Protestants claim that a set of sixty-six books, the (Protestant) Bible, is the sole infallible authority. For them, the Church is a friendly gathering of believers, all of whom have their own authority to interpret the Bible for themselves. (Although in many Protestant denominations, some believers have more "authority" than others.) Catholics, on the other hand, claim that God established His Church with divine authority passed on man-to-man, beginning with the original Apostles and continuing today through the bishops, to teach and understand the truth, which He gave to her in the deposit of Faith.

Based on this authority question, the ultimate claim this book makes is that the Protestant Reformation was not justified. Evidence for this view includes the fruits of the Reformation (endless divisions and doctrinal chaos), the natural conclusions of many of its claims (investigated in these pages), and the fact that reform *with-*

in the Church has been the only licit means for protesting abuses or bad practices.

I now ask that my Protestant sisters and brothers seriously consider how they might defend the Reformers' beliefs and their justifications for the Protestant Reformation. Modern-day spiritual descendants of the magisterial and the radical Reformers should seek to explain why this set of schisms were not schisms, or if they were, why these schisms are justified when no others before them were.

About two points, however, every Christian seeker of truth must be convinced: first, that the fullness of the portion of universal truth that Christ has revealed to us *can* indeed be discovered. (If it were otherwise, why would God go to the trouble of revealing Himself to us in the first place?) Since God desires that we know the truth, He must have made it possible for us to find it and for it to be preserved from falsehoods. Second, that there is no "secret knowledge" that saves us (remember, the Church squashed Gnosticism a long time ago). The final judgment will be of our hearts, not our knowledge base. Therefore, any search for Christian truth should be accompanied by a level of peace as we rest in the goodness of God our Father, Who loves us with an everlasting love.

Authority is God's Intention

Part of the appeal of the Protestant idea that the Bible is the ultimate authority is the seeming simplicity of it: any literate person can pick up the Bible and read it (once it has been translated into her language), interpreting it herself, and come to know divine truth. What could be better? And having it written down protects it from being corrupted like "tradition" can be. In our modern age of widespread literacy, interpreting the Bible for ourselves, meeting at our local church with other like-minded Christians, and electing our pastor (or unelecting him or her if deemed necessary) seems like a great way to be a Christian. Indeed, God can work through such ways of coming to know Him; He clearly has.

The problem with this conception of "the Church" and of the Christian Faith is that it is not how God *intended* us to know Him; He provided a means for *all* people to know Him, even before the relatively recent age of widespread literacy and the ability to print books—a time period that still represents the minority of the Christian epoch. God played a cruel joke on humanity if He intended all Christians throughout history to be like modern Protestants and know the truths of the Faith by "reading their Bibles" (which they didn't have, since Bibles were hand-written and extremely expensive, and which they couldn't have read anyway, because most were illiterate). God knew this reality, of course, which is why He entrusted the truth to rightful leaders of His Church, the men He poured his life into, the Apostles. Those then chose worthy men to succeed them, to preserve and deepen the understanding of this truth within Christ's Church by the divine power of the Holy Spirit. And of course, these successors to the Apostles have chosen at every turn to increase the laity's knowledge and understanding of the Bible . . . but with the proper, authoritative interpretation.

Christ has called all of us to be saints—men and women in every century, whether literate or illiterate, learned or ignorant. But He *hasn't* called us all to reinvent the Church for ourselves. He has given intellectual gifts to those He has called to be priests, bishops, and theologians so that, guided by Him, they could teach the Faith to all Christians, preach to those who had not yet heard of Christ, and defend the truth from the heresies that assaulted it in every age. Are the laity *also* called to teach, preach, and defend? By all means! But to define, detract, and detour? No.

Interpretation vs. Authority

Many Bible verses were cited in this book; however, relative to its length, the number of referenced verses is actually fairly small. Why? Wouldn't it have been better to "prove" all my arguments using the Bible? In my years of engaging in ecumenical dialogue with other Christians, one thing has become obvious: even seemingly clear biblical passages can be challenged and interpreted differently by well-meaning Christians who view them through their particular lens. This is the case among Catholics as well as Protestants. But since Protestants believe that the Bible is the ultimate authority, one has no way of demonstrating that a certain interpretation is indeed flawed. To most Protestants, their interpretation of the Bible *is* what the Bible says.

The truth is that the Bible can support multiple interpretive paradigms, even conflicting ones (just ask Luther, Calvin, Zwingli, and the Anabaptists). Listing verses and explaining how they are interpreted to support the Catholic paradigm only begs the question of who can rightly interpret the Bible. Instead, then, the focus of this book is on authority itself and the consequences of following the Protestant model of authority versus the Catholic one. We must get to the root of this fundamental question of authority and not waste time arguing about who is interpreting the Bible correctly on some specific issue. Though it is valuable to use verses to support a point, ultimately a Christian (or anyone) accepts or rejects a belief based on how he answers the more foundational question: Who is the authority here?

Jesus Himself gives us the confidence that in seeking Him we will find Him, Who is the Truth and ultimate Authority: "Ask and it will be given to you; seek and you will find; knock and the door will be opened to you. For everyone who asks, receives; and the one who seeks, finds; and to the one who knocks, the door will be opened" (Matt. 7:7–8). May Christ bless and guide your search to find and worship Him in spirit and in truth (see John 4:23), and may He unite us all as one in the fullness of the truth.

Notes

Chapter One: A Search for Truth

[1] Catechism of the Catholic Church (CCC):1472.

Chapter Two: Honest Self-Examination and Conversion

[1] Tom Brown, comment on Devin Rose "What You Said Sounds Good," St. Joseph's Vanguard and Our Lady's Train (blog), July 20, 2009, http://www.devinrose.heroicvirtuecreations.com/blog/2009/07/17/what-you-said-sounded-good/comment-page-1/#comment-57144.

Chapter Three: The Catholic Church in History

[1] Henry Graham, *Where We Got the Bible: Our Debt to the Catholic Church* (Charlotte: TAN Books & Publishers, 1994), III, 2.

[2] Patriarch Flavian of Constantinople to Pope Leo, 449 AD.

[3] Augustine, *Psalmus contra partem Donati*, 18 (A.D. 393), GCC 51.

[4] Pope Gregory I, Papal Bull of 570.

[5] See 1 Cor 12:12-31; Col 1:18; 2:18-20; Eph. 1:22-23; 3:19; 4:13.

[6] Vincent of Lerins, Notebooks 3:5.

[7] Catechism of the Catholic Church: 830.

[8] Irenaeus, *Against Heresies*, IV.26.

[9] Translated by Charles Gordon Browne and James Edward Swallow. From *Nicene and Post-Nicene Fathers*, Second Series, Vol. 7. Edited by Philip Schaff and Henry Wace. (Buffalo, NY: Christian Literature Publishing Co., 1894.) Revised and edited for New Advent by Kevin Knight. http://www.newadvent.org/fathers/310237.htm.

[10] Alister McGrath, *Christianity's Dangerous Idea: The Protestant Revolution--A History from the Sixteenth Century to the Twenty-First* (New York: HarperOne, 2007), 52.

Chapter Four: Reformation: Schism or Branches?

[1] Irenaeus, *Against Heresies*, IV.33:7-8.

[2] Irenaeus, *Against Heresies*, III.3:2.

[3] A diet was the general assembly of leaders of the Imperial States of the Holy Roman Empire.

[4] McGrath, *Christianity's Dangerous Idea*, 55.

[5] For more on Arius, see Chapter Three in the section on Ecumenical Councils.

[6] L'Osservatore Romano, Weekly Edition in English, 4 December 1996, page 11.

[7] *On the Divine Motherhood of Mary*, Weimer's The Works of Luther, English translation by Pelikan, Concordia, St. Louis, v. 7, p. 572.

[8] *Calvini Opera, Corpus Reformatorum*, Braunschweig-Berlin, 1863-1900, v. 45, p. 348, 35.

[9] *Luther's Works*, eds. Jaroslav Pelikan (vols. 1-30) & Helmut T. Lehmann (vols. 31-55), St. Louis: Concordia Pub. House (vols. 1-30); Philadelphia:

Fortress Press (vols. 31-55), 1955, v.22:23 / *Sermons on John*, chaps. 1-4 (1539).

[10] Pelikan, *ibid.*,v.45:206,212-3 / *That Jesus Christ was Born a Jew* (1523).

[11] *Harmony of Matthew, Mark & Luke*, sec. 39 (Geneva, 1562), vol. 2 / From *Calvin's Commentaries*, tr. William Pringle, Grand Rapids, MI: Eerdmans, 1949, p.215; on Matthew 13:55.

[12] Pringle, *ibid.*, vol. I, p. 107.

[13] Obermann, Heiko. *Luthers Werke.* Erlangen 1854, 32:282, 298, in Grisar, Hartmann. *Luther.* St. Louis 1915, 4:286 and 5:406, cited in Michael, Robert. *Holy Hatred: Christianity, Antisemitism, and the Holocaust.* New York: Palgrave Macmillan, 2006, p. 113.

[14] Martin Luther, *De Wette*, II, 459.

[15] CCC: 2089.

[16] Second Vatican Council, *Unitatis Redintegratio*, I.3, emphasis mine.

[17] *ibid.*

[18] http://en.wikipedia.org/wiki/A_New_Christianity_for_a_New_World.

[19] McGrath, *Christianity's Dangerous Idea*, 8.

[20] Warren Carroll, *The Building of Christendom: A History of Christendom, Volume 2* (Front Royal: Christendom Press, 2004), 85.

[21] Bonaventure, *The Life of St. Francis* (J.M. Dent, 1904), II.

Chapter Five: The Canon of Scripture

[1] Or, in the worst case, we are both wrong on the canon.

[2] Havey, F. (1907). African Synods. In The Catholic Encyclopedia. New York: Robert Appleton Company. Retrieved September 14, 2009 from New Advent: http://www.newadvent.org/cathen/01199a.htm.

[3] This does *not* mean that the Church "damned him to hell." Excommunication is a medicinal discipline intended to encourage the recipient to critically and prayerfully examine their teachings and actions so that they might return to full communion with Christ's Church. See Matt. 18:15-20 and 1 Cor. 5:1-13.

[4] From Luther's German translation of the New Testament, first edition: http://www.bible-researcher.com/antilegomena.html.

[5] *Luther's Works*, vol 35 (St. Louis: Concordia, 1963), 395-399.

[6] Modern-day Protestants, thankfully, tend to engage an opposite approach, submitting their *ideas* to *Scripture,* but this is only after accepting the canon crafted by the Reformers and thus influenced by their opinions.

[7] Vander Heeren, A. (1912). Septuagint Version. In The Catholic Encyclopedia. New York: Robert Appleton Company. Retrieved September 20, 2009 from New Advent: http://www.newadvent.org/cathen/13722a.htm.

[8] http://www.usccb.org/nab/bible/sirach/intro.htm.

[9] F. F. Bruce, *The Canon of Scripture* (Westmont: IVP Academic, 1988), 35.

[10] For some examples from the second and third centuries, see the writings of Ignatius of Antioch, Justin Martyr, Irenaeus, Tertullian, Clement of Alexandria, Origen, and Cyprian

[11] Catholic convert and apologist Tim Troutman sent this syllogism to me.

[12] John Calvin, *Institutes of the Christian Religion*, I.vii.1, 2, 5, John T. McNeill, ed., trans. Ford Lewis Battles, Philadelphia: Westminster Press, pp. 75-76, 80.

[13] R. C. Sproul, "Now That's a Good Question!" (Nelson, 1996), p. 81-82.

[14] McGrath, *Christianity's Dangerous Idea*, 79.

[15] From the second century, the Church Fathers Origen and Clement of Alexandria provide testimony that Jude is quoting from this legend.

Chapter Six: The Reformers' Legacy: Protestantism Today

[1] Russell Saltzman, "An Ecumenical Moment for One," *On the Square* (July 31, 2009), http://www.firstthings.com/onthesquare/2009/07/an-ecumenical-moment-for-one.

[2] Tom Wright, "The Americans Know This Will End in Schism," *The Times* (July 15, 2009), http://www.timesonline.co.uk/tol/comment/columnists/guest_contributors/article6710640.ece.

[3] http://www.nrlc.org/news/1999/NRL199/sween.html.

[4] Michael Spencer, "The Original Coming Collapse Posts," *Internet Monk* (March 10, 2009), http://www.internetmonk.com/archive/the-original-coming-evangelical-collapse-posts.

[5] McGrath, *Christianity's Dangerous Idea*, 219.

[6] McGrath, *Christianity's Dangerous Idea*, 403.

Chapter Seven: Protestant Objections to the Catholic Church

[1] O'Connor, J.B. (1910). St. Ignatius of Antioch. In The Catholic Encyclopedia. New York: Robert Appleton Company. Retrieved October 5, 2009 from New Advent: http://www.newadvent.org/cathen/07644a.htm.

[2] McGrath, *Christianity's Dangerous Idea*, 281.

[3] John Calvin, *Institutes of the Christian Religion*, Book 1, Chapter 13, 29.

[4] Maas, A. (1912). Versions of the Bible. In The Catholic Encyclopedia. New York: Robert Appleton Company. Retrieved October 7, 2009 from New Advent: http://www.newadvent.org/cathen/15367a.htm.

[5]

http://www.vatican.va/holy_father/benedict_xvi/audiences/2009/documents/hf_ben-xvi_aud_20090617_en.html.

[6] Alister McGrath, *Reformation Thought: An Introduction* (Oxford: Wiley-Blackwell, 2001), 165.

[7] The Epistle of Ignatius to the Smyrnaeans, VII, Roberts-Donaldson translation.

[8] Irenaeus, *Against Heresies*, I.10: 2.

Chapter Eight: The Sacraments

[1] Justin Martyr, *First Apology*, 61.

[2] Phillip Cary, "Sola Fide: Luther and Calvin," 2.

[3] McGrath, *Christianity's Dangerous Idea*, 262.

4 Phillip Cary, "Why Luther is Not Quite Protestant," 6–7.

5 Martin Luther, The Large Catechism, VIII, 4,
http://www.iclnet.org/pub/resources/text/wittenberg/luther/catechism
/web/cat-13.html

6 It should be noted here that Catholics do not believe in Luther's doctrine of sola fide, that we are justified by faith alone apart from love, but for the purposes of this argument, this difference is not directly relevant.

7 McGrath, *Christianity's Dangerous Idea*, 262.

8 Luther, The Large Catechism, XIIIA, 4,
http://www.iclnet.org/pub/resources/text/wittenberg/luther/catechism
/web/cat-13a.html.

9 Catechismus Concil. Trident., II, n. 4, ex S. August "De Catechizandis Rudibus."

10 There are some Protestant charismatic communities today that anoint with oil for healing.

11 Calvin, *Institutes* IV, 19, 18.

12 Ignatius of Antioch, *Letter to the Smyrnaeans*, 6:2–7:1.

13 Ambrose, *Concerning Repentance*, bk. 1, ch. 2.

14 CCC: 1536, 1538.

15 Augustine, To Generosus, Epistle 53:2.

16 Clement, *Letter to the Corinthians*, I, 42–44.

17 Joseph Cardinal Ratzinger, *Called to Communion*, 114–115.

Chapter Nine: Tradition

[1] Pope Benedict XVI, Wednesday audience, May 4, 2006, Zenit translation.

[2] G. Joyce, "Revelation," In *The Catholic Encyclopedia*. (New York: Robert Appleton, 1912. Retrieved November 12, 2009 from New Advent, http://www.newadvent.org/cathen/13001a.htm.

[3] *Westminster Confession of Faith*, I.VI.

[4] Note that Mormons reject this Tradition. They believe that ongoing public revelation can occur and has occurred since the 1820s, when God allegedly reestablished the Church through Joseph Smith and gave him the *Book of Mormon* as "another testament of Jesus Christ."

[5] Council of Trent, *Decree on Sacred Scripture and Tradition*: Denziger 783 [1501]).

[6] Irenaeus, *Against Heresies*, III.3:4.

[7] Mark Noll, *The Scandal of the Evangelical Mind* (Grand Rapids: Eerdmans, 1995), 63.

[8] William Webster, *The Church of Rome at the Bar of History* (Carlisle, Pennsylvania: Banner of Truth, 1997), 134.

[9] J. Sollier, "The Communion of Saints," In *The Catholic Encyclopedia*. (New York: Robert Appleton, 1908). Retrieved November 28, 2009 from New Advent, http://www.newadvent.org/cathen/04171a.htm.

[10] See 2 Maccabees 12:38–46.

Chapter Ten: The Scriptures

[1] McGrath, *Christianity's Dangerous Idea*, 69–70.

[2] Keith Mathison, "Solo Scriptura: The Difference a Vowel Makes" 25–29,
http://www.modernreformation.org/default.php?page=articledisplay&var1=ArtRead&var2=19&var3=authorbio&var4=AutRes&var5=17.

[3] McGrath, *Christianity's Dangerous Idea*, 221.

[4] Martin Luther, *The Bondage of the Will*, (tr. Henry Cole (Grand Rapids, MI: Baker Book House, 1976), 25-7, 29 (emphasis in original)

[5] see *Dei Verbum*, 12.

Index

Spong, John Shelby, 58

Sproul, R.C., 78

sterilization, 89, 90

Summa Theologiae, 142

Syriac, 83, 102

The Assumption of Moses, 83

The Jesus Seminar, 58

Therese of Lisieux, 25

Thomas Aquinas, 44, 142

Titus, 31

Tobit, 66, 72

tradition, 16, 22, 23, 24, 42, 49, 80, 86, 119, 121, 135, 140, 141, 142, 149, 155, 160

Tradition, 6, 22, 28, 32, 33, 49, 50, 54, 80, 98, 107, 124, 135, 136, 138, 140, 155, 170

transubstantiation, 125

Trent, 56, 69, 170

trilingual heresy, 102

Trinity, 52, 80, 86, 103, 105, 113, 120, 121

Troutman, Tim, 166

Unitatis Redintegratio, 56, 165

vernacular, 103

Vincent of Lerins, 35, 163

virginity, 39, 40, 53, 54, 98, 136

Webster, William, 142

Westminster, 137, 167, 170

Williams, Rowan, 88

Wisdom, 66

Wittenberg, 58, 80

Wright, N.T., 88

Zwingli, Ulrich, 48, 151

CPSIA information can be obtained at www.ICGtesting.com
Printed in the USA
LVOW101702130212

268493LV00011B/122/P